International Perspectives in Geography
AJG Library 4

Editor in Chief:
Noritaka Yagasaki, Japan

More information about this series at
http://www.springer.com/series/10223

Aims and Scope:

The AJG Library is published by Springer under the auspices of the Association of Japanese Geographers. This is a scholarly series of international standing. Given the multidisciplinary nature of geography, the objective of the series is to provide an invaluable source of information not only for geographers, but also for students, researchers, teachers, administrators, and professionals outside the discipline. Strong emphasis is placed on the theoretical and empirical understanding of the changing relationships between nature and human activities. The overall aim of the series is to provide readers throughout the world with stimulating and up-to-date scientific outcomes mainly by Japanese and other Asian geographers. Thus, an "Asian" flavor different from the Western way of thinking may be reflected in this series. The AJG Library will be available both in print and online via SpringerLink.

About the AJG

The Association of Japanese Geographers (AJG), founded in 1925, is one of the largest and leading organizations on geographical research in Asia and the Pacific Rim today, with around 3000 members. AJG is devoted to promoting research on various aspects of human and physical geography and contributing to academic development through exchanges of information and knowledge with relevant internal and external academic communities. Members are tackling contemporary issues such as global warming, air/water pollution, natural disasters, rapid urbanization, irregular land-use changes, and regional disparities through comprehensive investigation into the earth and its people. In addition, to make the next generation aware of these academic achievements, the members are engaged in teaching and outreach activities of spreading geographical awareness. With the recent developments and much improved international linkages, AJG launches the publication of the AJG Library series in 2012.

Editorial Board:

Kenta Yamamoto

The Agglomeration of the Animation Industry in East Asia

 Springer

Kenta Yamamoto
Kokugakuin University
Tokyo, Japan

ISSN 2197-7798   ISSN 2197-7801 (electronic)
ISBN 978-4-431-55092-1   ISBN 978-4-431-55093-8 (eBook)
DOI 10.1007/978-4-431-55093-8
Springer Tokyo Heidelberg New York Dordrecht London

Library of Congress Control Number: 2014944072

Printed on acid-free paper

Springer is part of Springer Science+Business Media (www.springer.com)

Preface

The social changes that swept industrialized countries in the second half of the twentieth century, especially their metropolitan areas, were described in a variety of ways by those living through them. Daniel Bell (1973), an American sociologist, identified these changes as heralding "the coming of the post-industrial society." The economist John Kenneth Galbraith (1977) saw them as representative of "the Age of Uncertainty." In slight contrast, Alvin Toffler (1980), a futurist, described them collectively as "the Third Wave." In all of these cases, it is clear that the scholars were convinced of the significance of the social changes taking place around them. Indeed, the nature of the city was undergoing a remarkable transformation.

Manufacturing industries had dominated the growth of urban economies since the Industrial Revolution. Toward the end of the 1960s, however, the number of industrial laborers began to shrink rapidly in both New York and London. This industrial structural change contributed to the rise of inner-city problems in the 1970s. Starting in 1980, however, populations and employment rates in New York and London began to recover from their declines. One sector that was significantly involved in this recovery was business services, including the field of international finance. Saskia Sassen (1991) focused on the role of these new players and reported on the related structural changes that affected urban economies following economic globalization. In terms of employment numbers, business services had taken the place of the manufacturing sector as a promoter of the urban economy by the early 1990s.

John Friedmann, who pointed out the necessity of understanding urbanization in the context of the world economy (Friedmann and Wolff 1982), hypothesized that the creation and dissemination of culture and information would become a subfunction of metropolises in the emerging world city (Friedmann 1986). According to this theory, metropolises in developed countries become the primary bases for administration, provision of services, and transmission of information under a global economic structure.

Advances in information technology sustained the economic globalization of the metropolises. These innovations, which began in the 1980s and accelerated in the late 1990s, led to the birth of Internet-related industries as a subfield of business services. The importance of the role of this new sector in the continued predominance of business services as a promoter of urban economies increased at the end of the last century. Advanced information industries tended to concentrate in central areas of metropolises. One reason for this tendency is that these industries were based on widely and mutually complementary labor divisions, which enabled various participants in the field to form complex networks based on their physical proximity. Another reason is that the social divisions within the labor networks in the metropolises acted as a creative and developmental generator of culture within the global economy.

The revitalization of urban economies in highly developed countries in the 1980s promoted "culture" as a new player in urban economics alongside business services and information-related industries in the 1990s. This is one aspect of a paradigm shift toward a new economic geography, which Philip Crang (1997) called a "cultural turn." Now, needless to say, we cannot avoid including culture as an economic element that allows us to understand the activities of economic players on global and local scales in contemporary urban economies. At this point, the culture-creation function that Friedmann predicted in 1986 is becoming more and more important in the metropolises of advanced countries.

In this context, this book focuses on the animation industry, a major Japanese cultural industry, and on the agglomerated structure of that industry. Animation studios are most highly concentrated in Tokyo. As in the information industry, the agglomeration of animation studios in Tokyo is explained on the basis of transactions and the sharing of labor among the studios. In addition, the emerging agglomerated structure of the animation industry, not only in Tokyo, but also in Seoul and Shanghai, has developed under the influence of a system of international division of labor involving overseas animation industries, especially Japanese and Western companies. With an understanding of the generality and regionality of the agglomeration of the animation industry, this book compares the characteristics of the agglomeration process in the three metropolises of Tokyo, Seoul, and Shanghai. Our analysis is expanded to the relationship between the agglomerated structure and the workers as assessed through a survey about the characteristics of the labor market and the career-formation processes of those workers.

Tokyo, Japan   Kenta Yamamoto

References

Bell D (1973) The coming of post-industrial society. Basic Books, New York
Crang P (1997) Cultural turns and the (re)constitution of economic geography. In: Lee R, Wills J (eds) Geography of economies. Arnold, New York
Friedmann J (1986) The world city hypothesis. Dev Change 17:69–84
Friedmann J, Wolff G (1982) World city formation: an agenda for research and action. Int J Urban Reg Res 6:309–344
Galbraith JK (1977) The age of uncertainty. Houghton Mifflin Company, Boston
Sassen S (1991) The global city: New York, London, Tokyo. Princeton University Press, New Jersey
Toffler A (1980) The third wave. William Morrow and Company, New York

Acknowledgments

This book is based on my doctoral thesis presented to Tohoku University in 2009. First, I express my appreciation to my advisor, Professor Masateru Hino, and my friends in the Department of Geography, Tohoku University, for their tutelage, advice, and discussions. Some chapters in this book are based on my investigations from when I was in the Department of Human Geography of The University of Tokyo as a postdoctoral researcher, and I would also like to thank Professor Yoshio Arai and my Department of Human Geography colleagues.

I also would like to recognize a number of individuals who helped me with various aspects of my research. Animation industry participants in Japan, South Korea, and China, especially Studio M members, cooperated with my research over the long term. I could not have produced any writing about this industry without their kind help, and so they have my greatest gratitude.

I would like to thank many South Korean and Chinese scholars for assisting with my survey in their countries. Professor Changwan Han at Sejong University, Professor Wansoo Joo at the Korea National University of Arts, Professor Gyoungil Ko at Sangmyung University, and Professor Hwanyeong Jeong and his students, including Professor Jeong Sokho, in the Department of Geography at Kongju National University helped me when I collected data about the South Korean animation industry. South Korea was my first overseas survey field, and they gave me invaluable guidance on how to conduct research in foreign countries. Professor De Wang, Professor Zhengsheng Yin, and Mr. Li Ma at Tongjin University, and Professor Jinfeng Chu, Mr. Feng Gao, Ms. Nana Li, and Mr. Xiande Li along with members of the Geography Department at Shanghai Normal University helped me with my research in Shanghai in 2007. I was able to obtain valuable data about the animation studios located in the Shanghai region through their considerable contributions.

And thank you to my dear friends Mr. Shinnosuke Iijima and Mr. Derek Lattimer for their helpful advice and great support. I could not have completed this book without their dedicated efforts, and they have my deep appreciation and gratitude.

Chapters published in this book were supported by the following grants. A part of this investigation was funded by a Grant-in-Aid for Scientific Research (C) (No. 23320187) from the Japan Society for the Promotion of Science (JSPS), and a

Grant-in-Aid for JSPS Research Fellowships for Young Scientists (No. 20-3145). And for the publication of this book, the International Perspectives in Geography: AJG Library was especially supportive.

Finally, I would like to thank my family for supporting my research activities for many years. I dedicate this book to my grandfather, Masashiro, who passed away in 2012.

Contents

Chapter 1
Academic Context of the Animation Industry

Abstract Previous studies on cultural and content industries are reviewed to explain the perspective of this study. To clarify the agglomerated structure of the animation industry, examples of networks built on different spatial scales are provided, such as division of labor among regions, transactional relationships among studios, and interpersonal relationships among workers. In addition, animation industry studies, not only in Japan, but also in South Korea and China, are described to provide background context for the following chapters.

Keywords Content industry • Cultural industry • Network

1.1 Introduction

Given the dramatic advances in the transportation and information technologies that have allowed the world economy to globalize over the last few decades, experts have begun to speculate on whether the world is now "flat" (Friedman 2007) or perhaps "spiky" (Florida 2008). Previous thinkers supposed that globalization would lead to creative workers being drawn to specific cities and regions. In reality, now more than ever, talented people can do their creative work wherever they are. Current transportation technology can provide sushi to people living at the foot of the Alps, while new information technology enables tourists boating on the Amazon River to check the yen exchange rate in real time. These technologies instantaneously connect people around the world by helping people who do not live in close proximity to keep in touch. Thus people can choose where they want to live and still be able to build connections with other people. For this reason, it might be said that the world has become flat. However, Florida (2002, 2005) pointed out the power of "the three Ts"—technology, talent, and tolerance—which attract people and economic growth to particular regions and create spikes in the global economy.

Cultural industries requiring creativity sustained by the three Ts—especially in industrialized countries—are regarded as leaders of culture and economics for the next generation and therefore attract the attention of scholars (e.g., Scott 2000;

© Springer Japan 2014
K. Yamamoto, *The Agglomeration of the Animation Industry in East Asia*,
International Perspectives in Geography: AJG Library 4,
DOI 10.1007/978-4-431-55093-8_1

Power 2002; Clark 2003; Power and Scott 2004; Hesmondhalgh 2007; Howkins 2007; Kong and O'Connor 2009; Hesmondhalgh and Baker 2011). In fact, the present spatial distribution of certain cultural industries, especially the content industry,[1] shows that people who work in these industries tend to congregate in specific areas. For example, studios that produce movies, music, and print media are located in major metropolises like New York, London, Paris, and Tokyo (e.g., Scott 2000; Gibson et al. 2002; Abrahamson 2004). In our focus on the Japanese animation industry, we find that more than 78 % of Japanese animation studios are located in Tokyo, which demonstrates its monopolistic position in the Japanese animation industry (see Chap. 2).

A reason for this agglomeration is that metropolises consist of multiple industrial clusters in close proximity with each other, which leads to synergistic effects on the creativity in the industry. Both Throsby (2001) and Pratt (1997) defined cultural industries according to a concentric circles model with each industry centered on a creative "core" according to Throsby's theory, and with a productive system consisting of four essentially different industrial groups according to Pratt's theory. These definitions show that the essence of a cultural industry is to create new cultural value through interlocking relationships involving several industries. Throsby described these relationships as "a concentric-circles model of the cultural industries, with the arts lying at the center, and with other industries forming layers or circles located around the core, extending further outwards (with) the use of creative ideas" and suggested that this model provides the cultural industry with "a wider production context" (Throsby 2001, p. 113). This characteristic and fundamental structure of cultural industries can be seen in the "cultural-products industrial districts," as described by Scott (2004) in his experimental study focusing on the characteristics of spaces that produce cultural products. Cultural industries cannot run independently; they rely on mutually complementary relationships between neighboring industries according to the business outcome, thus jointly forming cultural-products industrial districts, i.e., cultural industry clusters. Metropolises are essential for the expression of creativity in certain cultural industries.

1.2 Characteristics of the Content Industry

This study focuses on the content industry, which is a set of growing industries in modern metropolises, and especially on the animation industry, one of the major providers of Japanese pop culture. Although the content industry tends to be

---

[1] The Ministry of Economy, Trade and Industry defines "content" as "something that affects human emotion" (2008, p. 6) and the "content industry" as "the industry sustaining production and distribution in the field of motion pictures (i.e., film and animation), music, games, and books" (2011, p. 3). According to these descriptions, the content industry falls into the categories of "media and related industries" and "specialized design services" in the cultural-products industrial districts of Scott's theory (Scott 2004). Especially in Japan, the animation industry attracts attention as one of the global economy's highly competitive content industries (Ministry of Economy, Trade and Industry 2008, 2011).

agglomerated in metropolises, its production output, such as films, music, and animated pictures, can be consumed both domestically and, in some cases, internationally.

Previous studies on content industries have identified two characteristics of the creative process unique to these industries. The first is that the division of labor has been highly developed to encourage growth in the form of international specialization. The other is that the skills of individual workers and the local networks among them are important to the labor market in the industry.

1.2.1 Previous Studies About the Creative Process

In studies on the international division of labor, overseas transfer of work from the American film industry is a popular topic (e.g., Miller and Leger 2001; Elmer and Gasher 2005). The need for this transfer and division of labor is generally regarded as a "runaway production problem" in the industry, and two factors are indicated as its causes. The first is decreased investment, which leads US studios to order overseas production for the sake of cost reduction and increased profitability. The other is that studios can take advantage of various types of support in foreign countries whose governments implement policies that promote industrial endeavors.

For example, Goldsmith and O'Regan (2003) used "studio complexes" and industrial promotion in major cities in Australia and Canada to explain how government support of film production attracts business from the American movie industry.[2] Studio complexes provide the services required to produce the large volumes of work requested by the studios' clients within their production facilities. In addition, Govil (2005) reported that the popularization of high-speed Internet and the rise of the computer graphics industry, both of which have expanded rapidly in Mumbai, India, are the leading factors that have driven Mumbai's rise as a major special effects production base for Hollywood. Coe (2001) showed that governmental support, in such forms as funding aid, continuous tax deduction, and capital investment in large quantities, as well as the clustering of related industries, have led to an initial agglomeration in Vancouver of studios that originated in Hollywood. In addition, Coe also pointed out that the characteristic structure of the Vancouver film industry was based on huge investments of American capital, a large number of small and local studios, and a labor force sustained by project-to-project labor associations. Production studios in Vancouver are dependent on American studios and are therefore affected and controlled by them.

---

[2]A "studio complex" is a combination of facilities and zones where people can film movies on a variety of scales. It has four primary functions: (1) acoustic facilities available for any type of filming; (2) services sustaining the production and postproduction departments; (3) filming facilities for several types of outdoor locations; and (4) services sustaining the large volume of production financially supported by foreign capital.

On the other hand, Scott and Pope (2007) focused on the US government's reaction to a hollowing out of investment in the American film industry. They noted that policies regarding tax benefits under discussion by the California state government may delay the consequent hollowing out of the film industry temporarily, but effectively.

In summary, the formation of a local film industry is heavily dependent on the relationship with its client country based on the international division of labor. To clarify the process of agglomeration in the content industry, it is therefore necessary to discuss the division of the production process, correspondence with subcontracted workers in foreign countries, and the structures formed during development of the industry in those countries.

1.2.2   Research on Workers

Several previous studies have underscored the second abovementioned characteristic of the content industry, namely, the value of the individuals and of the relationships among them that sustain production within the industry. For example, Coe (2000) observed that different local producers in the Vancouver film industry use different connections based on their own personal networks to produce their films according to the spatial scale of the targeted market. This study also clarified that the connections between nations, regions, and local groups do not exist independently, but are mutually linked, and that the content-producing ability of producers is strongly defined by how deeply the producer is embedded into these connections.

Additionally, some studies have pointed out the importance of networks between workers in the content industry. Because of an interest in the career formation of designers, Vinodrai (2006) conducted detailed interviews with 60 designers in Toronto, the results of which suggest that coworkers who overlap in the same department at the same time affect one another's careers and career changes. They learn techniques and other relevant information through relationships with each other, and their reputations are developed and reinforced through relationships with former colleagues. Moreover, relationships and networks between designers function as employment agencies, as designers rely on their networks for job-searching purposes as well. In other words, workers stabilize their working environments by building networks (Blair 2003) and even by forming studios with their coworkers, which in turn affects their self-identification (Bain 2004, 2005).

In the Japanese animation industry, it is important to validate the production ability of the studios while also building relationships within them. These conditions are realized through personal connections, as was shown by Hanzawa (2001). Hara (2005) also backed up this theory with his own research, in which he conducted interview surveys with workers and a behavioral observation with a producer over 1 week. His results showed that the human networks built around producers encourage the integration of the various industrial clusters located in Tokyo, including animation, computer graphics, and video game studios, which in turn enables the studios to utilize 3D (three dimensional) computer graphics technologies to keep the quality of their products high even under strict deadlines and financial limitations.

These studies show that the contribution of human networks around specific persons can accelerate industrial development. These persons do not have these networks before they enter the field; rather, they build these networks during their working tenures. As Drake (2003) asserted, it is necessary to discuss the relationship between working spaces and the activities of creative persons to uncover the spatial structure of the creative industries. Understanding the social networks that connect talented people through their daily activities and the behavior of workers at the studios is fundamental to clarifying how industrial development can be based on networks of workers.

1.2.3 Geographical Studies on the Content Industry in Japan

In Japan, geographical studies on the content industry have accumulated since 2000, usually centered on one of two perspectives. The first concerns the factors contributing to industrial agglomeration in metropolises and how these factors affect each other to influence the structure of the industry. The other perspective concerns the suggestion that cities may be able to promote the development of a local content industry through shifts in their production and distribution systems based on advanced information technologies.

Some studies on the content industry's agglomeration in metropolises have focused specifically on the animation industry (e.g., Hanzawa 2001; Hara 2005). These studies have proposed various factors as the primary element responsible for agglomeration. These factors include the presence of other types of industrial clusters in metropolises, which encourage innovative production and the circulation of capital and human resources (Hara 2005); the necessity of proximity to the targeted market; and time compression in the distribution channels (Hanzawa 2001). Other studies have also indicated the role of the need for proximity between companies and technology professionals in encouraging agglomeration in the information industry (Arai et al. 2004), as well as the importance of unofficial opportunities for communication between workers and studios (Furukawa 2010).

Although most content industries agglomerate in metropolises, some studies indicate the possibility of the promotion and development of content industries in smaller cities. For example, Masubuchi researched the independent music industry in Okinawa (Masubuchi 2005) and the TV program production industry in Hokkaido (Masubuchi 2007), showing how these industries provide opportunities for creative people who, in most cases, would otherwise leave these smaller cities to work in metropolises like Tokyo. In his research, he recognized that the major production sites and markets for the content industry are metropolises, yet he insists that a shift in the production and distribution systems along with the aid of modern information technology could enable the content industry to operate in smaller cities.

Government support and the presence of human networks would be required for smaller cities to promote this industry and create new local opportunities for jobs and creative actualization. Hanzawa (2005) also pointed out the possibility of decentralization of the industry in his research concerning the domestic division of labor in the Japanese video game industry.

1.3 Studies of the Animation Industry

Unlike the multimedia and Web industries, which have developed only recently, but at a rapid pace, the animation industry in Tokyo has been developing since the 1960s, when animation was first broadcast on national TV. Most animation studios are now based in Tokyo, and the pattern of the division of labor among studios is well developed. Hence, the structure needed to produce this specific kind of creativity has also been developing over time. Even though the digitization in the Japanese animation industry has progressed, the analog process, which is characterized by such features as hand-drawn pictures by creative workers, face-to-face communication, and the direct delivery of half-finished products, still occupies an important role in the production process. This means that the social relationships between coworkers as well as their working conditions are expected to retain a strong influence on the spatial function of the studio where the creative workers gather. The animation industry has an unusual industrial structure. This section introduces some important studies and background knowledge.

The animation industry was already developing before Mickey Mouse first appeared on screen steering a steamship. Although this industry is nearly 100 years old, its history has only recently received recognition as a research subject. One of the earliest studies focusing on the spatial characteristics of companies and laborers' activities in the industry is by Scott (1988a), who explored the reproduction of local labor markets in the animation industry in Los Angeles. Scott chose 270 workers from IATSE 839,[3] a labor union in the animation industry, and analyzed the correlation between the locations of their studios and the residences of the workers with the types of jobs they performed and the payment system in the industry. Scott observed that their employment conditions were highly unstable and that workers were typically unemployed for 3 months out of a given year. Studios satisfied their labor needs by locating their production facilities in areas with high population densities of younger, single workers to ensure that there were sufficient workers living nearby.

After the pioneering study by Scott, there has been little research on the spatial characteristics of the animation industry. One of the reasons for this stems from the

---

[3]The Animation Guild and Affiliated Optical Electronic and Graphic Arts, Local 839 of the International Alliance of Theatrical Stage Employees and Moving Picture Technicians, Artists and Allied Crafts of the United States, its Territories and Canada, American Federation of Labor-Congress of Industrial Organizations/Canadian Labour Congress (IATSE 839) is the best-known labor union for animation creators and directors on the west coast of the United States.

difficulty in obtaining statistical data specifically for the animation industry, as the animation industry is often treated as part of the TV or film industry. For example, as the American film industry began to recognize the development of the runaway production problem throughout the 1990s, Lent (1998) specifically focused on the animation industry as part of the film industry and described how the phenomenon emerged in the American animation industry as a result of labor costs being higher in the home (headquarters) countries than in the processing countries. Yet even his challenging analysis was based on interviews at animation production studios rather than on statistical data.

Japan, South Korea, and China are the most prolific regions of animation production in East Asia; their productivity is sustained by the international division of labor connecting them. In South Korea, the major focus of animation industry studies has been the nature of the rapid structural transformations that occurred around 2000, as well as industrial expansion (e.g., Korea Culture and Contents Agency 2004; Korea Creative Content Agency 2010), future development (e.g., Kim 2001; You and Cha 2004), changes in production because of advances in digitization technology (Han 2005; Shin 2002), and so on. Chinese studies, in contrast, are mostly evaluations of policy or policy proposals, such as a report about the current national market (Lu 2011), suggestions for directing such a market (Qin 2006; Lu et al. 2011), and a proposal to abandon the existing industrial structure with its heavy reliance on overseas studios (Editorial Board of China Animation Yearbook 2007; Development and Reform Center for China's State Administration of Radio, Film and Television 2006). In this respect, the studies on the animation industry in South Korea and China have touched only the tip of the iceberg, given that the industry has experienced rapid development despite the fact that studies are yet to trace the formation of spatial structures in the industry.

In Japan, however, studies from a geographic perspective based on empirical methods have accumulated. Hanzawa (2001) and Hara (2005) have conducted representative studies. Hanzawa (2001) focused on the characteristics of the transactional relationships between firms to explain the structure of agglomeration in the animation industry. According to his study, firms emphasize business acumen and trustworthiness when choosing their partner companies, and gathering information through rumors or reputation as advertised on social networks is important to ensure such criteria. Hara (2005) had a more narrow focus in his study of the animation industry, concentrating on the project management of an animation series. The projects were accomplished through the cooperation of three elements: various industrial clusters in Tokyo, skillful workers, and producer networks connecting the first two elements. Hara also emphasized the importance of continuous capital investments, which enable the animation industry agglomerates in Tokyo to obtain the resources they require.

In summary, previous studies on the animation industry in Japan have mentioned the importance of the networks formed by participants in the industry, such as firms and workers, and the agglomerated structure of the animation industry in Tokyo, but they have insufficiently discussed the relationship between the creativity found in the metropolises and the daily activities of participants in the industry.

1.4   Overview of Agglomeration Theory Since the 1980s

Since the 1980s, and especially since the theory of Piore and Sable (1984) was published, interest in industrial agglomeration has been based on the question of how regions survive in competition with other regions in a context of globalization and the expansion of market instability in a post-mass-production era. Studies have identified an agglomeration structure composed of horizontal and vertical networks of small and medium-sized enterprises based on flexible specialization. There are two main interpretations of the reasons why these networks are built: one stems from the drive toward economic rationality through such goals as reducing transaction costs, and the other stems from the desire for knowledge, creativity, and innovation as a form of social capital.

Scott (1988b) presented one of the representative studies emphasizing the external economic motivations for agglomeration. He blends original agglomeration theory with Piore and Sable's flexible specialization theory, calling the result "new industrial spaces." The focus of his theory is transactions among enterprises, and he points out that social divisions of labor develop among businesses to allow them to avoid losses from unstable market demands. This social division of labor is undertaken by specialized small and medium-sized enterprises, which tend to concentrate in certain places to reduce linkage costs (specifically, transaction and transportation costs).

Under the mass production structure, major companies promote operation outsourcing and diversify risks to avoid losses from instability in the market. Contractors take on parts of the production processes of major companies exclusively. These transactional relationships among individual firms are fixed and closed to other business groups. On the other hand, contractors may also pursue transactional relationships with some clients and build interdependent and complementary relationships while selling labor and technology to their clients under the theory of new industrial spaces. Client companies flexibly choose contractors according to their current needs. Horizontal transactional relationships are built among contractors that perform the same production processes. Thus companies can accommodate their transactions to fit market trends, and transactional relationships among companies are open to other potential business partners. This is the first agglomeration theory. Studies supporting this agglomeration theory attribute agglomeration to economic factors.

Studies supporting the second agglomeration theory, on the other hand, have mainly appeared since the mid-1990s. These studies employ concepts and methods from social science, such as the concept of a "cultural turn" (Crang 1997, p. 3), to economic geography, interpreting agglomeration in terms of such key concepts as milieu, knowledge creation, innovation, and learning.

Camagni (1991), for example, emphasized that the benefits that inspire agglomeration are proximity to others with similar cultural and psychological attitudes, interpersonal contact, and ease of cooperation and information exchange. Camagni also emphasized that firms can achieve innovation through these benefits. Saxenian (1994) focused on Silicon Valley and Route 128, two regions both known as centers of high-tech industry, and observed that industries in the former region are rapidly growing while the industries in the latter are relatively stagnating or declining. As the reason for the rise of Silicon Valley, Saxenian suggested the importance of a "regional network-based industrial system" (p. 2) formed around Silicon Valley. In this system, workers have high mobility and firms can utilize flexible and specialized labor forces in the region. Firms also find it easy to build formal and informal cooperative relationships with other firms. These social relationships allow firms to acquire a competitive technological advantage over firms located in other regions. These social relationships are collectively called the "milieu."

Florida (1995) also compared industrial systems in different types of regions: specifically, mass production regions and learning regions. The structure of mass production regions is characterized by the integration of firms in the region. Firms located in mass production regions demand quantity of production, integrate various production processes into themselves, and completely control workers in their integrated production departments to maintain quality and quantity of production. The structure of learning regions, on the other hand, is characterized by a network-type organization consisting of codependent relationships among participants: firms outsource even those departments that are indispensable for production. Although this structure incorporates social division of labor among firms and is the same as that described in Scott's new industrial space theory, Florida pointed out that forming a competitive advantage through knowledge creation is a factor promoting the division of labor, while Scott emphasized its usefulness in reducing transaction costs. Workers in learning regions have opportunities for learning and information exchange in the region and demand opportunities to apply their knowledge on the production site.[4] Because of keen competition with other regions, regions that are integrated into the global economy must achieve knowledge creation unceasingly. The flexible and dynamic networks among workers and firms in learning regions encourage continuous knowledge creation as a source of competitive advantage.

Capello (1999) argued that there is a difference between the concepts of learning and collective learning, and also suggested the importance of the networks and knowledge creation formed in a particular region. Capello also pointed out that creative knowledge accumulates around a firm, and that only cooperating firms can use the accumulated knowledge. In other words, the process of accumulating and using knowledge is collective learning, and these relationships among cooperating firms give insiders a competitive advantage in that only these insiders can utilize the knowledge. Keeble et al. (1999) indicated the importance of social, economic, and political environments, referred to as "institutional thickness," for collective learning and satisfaction with innovation throughout the process by workers in the region.[5] Institutional thickness plays a role in external economy for firms by promoting agglomeration and increasing the likelihood of innovation.

---

[4] Florida (2002, 2005) regards these workers as belonging to the "creative class."

[5] Institutional thickness is determined by various factors, including political support, infrastructure, venture capital, universities that produce workers with high levels of skill and knowledge, places for formal and informal information exchange among firms, and related industries providing specialized services.

This completes our review of some recent arguments concerning industrial agglomeration, especially in the context of cultural turns. These studies have focused on how regions gain a competitive advantage and create new products and have sought to identify the characteristics of regions that do so. For example, firms located in these regions possess a competitive advantage through their use of local networks, which is an attraction for other firms that are starting up or moving and choosing a new location, thus promoting agglomeration. Porter (2008) explained the importance of firm location and the effect of widening regional differences on global competitiveness among firms: the profits acquired through globalization are not distributed equally among regions. Thus, many previous studies have emphasized localization as a survival strategy for regions.

These regional differences are not necessarily because the networks are established in specific places. Regions of industrial agglomeration embedded in the global production system have their own roles to play, and each region changes its own social and economic structures. After identifying and describing four types of regional networks, namely, the Marshallian industrial district, hub-and-spoke district, satellite platform district, and state-centered district, Marksen (1996) pointed out that "improving cooperative relationships and building networks that reach outside of the region[6] may prove more productive for some localities than concentrating on indigenous firms" (Marksen 1996, p. 310).

Structural changes in the industrial regions brought on by globalization have also given new roles to these regions in the global network. A study by Saxenian (2006) focused on Taiwan and Israel—both of which have become new centers of the information technology industry—as well as China and India—both of which are now becoming new centers of the high-tech industry. Within their own geographic contexts, these regions all have similar structures. As in Silicon Valley, many firms in each of these regions have built unofficial and flexible networks among competitive and cooperative firms, as previously indicated by Saxenian (1994). This Silicon Valley-style system was introduced into each region by "Argonauts"—a term used to describe entrepreneurs who acquired their technical and management know-how in Silicon Valley. Connections among these regions and with Silicon Valley are also maintained by these Argonauts. With regard to these networks that have formed among the regions, Saxenian reported that "the proliferation of cross-border venture capitalists and start-ups underscores the advantages of combining the specialized and complementary capabilities of producers located in distant regions" (Saxenian 2006, p. 330).

As described above, the industrial structures in regions that have opened themselves to the global economy are formed through the interaction between global and local networks. Thus, it is necessary to analyze both global and local networks to understand the structure of each region. Moreover, it is necessary to focus on the relationships between industrial agglomerations and the activities of workers

---

[6]These regions can be categorized as a hub-and-spoke district and a satellite platform district, respectively. Each has been able to become a new center in the international division of labor by attracting large-scale transnational enterprise.

because, as Florida (2002) emphasized, a creative person who partially exists in the world plays an important role in the economic development of his or her region.

1.5 Focus and Outline of This Book

This chapter has introduced several previous studies about site selection in the content industry. The content industry consists of various spatial networks that are part of the production process and that operate in both global and local spaces. It is therefore necessary to identify each network built upon a specific space to understand the overall spatial structure of the content industry. There are three characteristic factors that are important and necessary elements for a studio's site selection: the interaction of participants' transactional relationships at sites where the industry agglomerates, the workers' networks, and the structure of the international division of labor.

On the basis of the abovementioned studies, I have researched industrial agglomeration in metropolises and the system of international division of labor that has evolved in the animation industry (Yamamoto 2007, 2008, 2009). This book expands the scope of my previous studies to both vertical transactional relationships between studios and the horizontal division of labor relationships, the characteristics of the labor market, the career paths of workers in the industry, and the effects of all these elements on agglomeration. I focus on the relationships between participants in the production process within the animation industry. The factors behind the observed industrial agglomeration and the structure of this agglomeration will be examined.

Hence, the book covers not only Tokyo, the capital of the animation industry, but also some other East Asian cities such as Seoul, South Korea, and Shanghai, China, both of which have experienced agglomeration of the animation industry. These local industries have been developed through the building of relationships with Japanese and Western animation studios. Both cities have served as production bases where the international division of labor for labor-intensive processes is put into practice. Therefore, discussing Seoul and Shanghai as case studies can be helpful in clarifying the regionality and the generality of agglomeration in the animation industry.

This book consists of seven chapters. Chapters 2, 3, and 4 are based on my studies in 2007, 2008, and 2009, respectively. Chapter 2 attempts to provide an accurate picture of the agglomeration of the animation industry in Tokyo and the factors leading to this agglomeration. Since the industrialization of Tokyo began in 1961, transactional relationships and the division of labor between the Japanese animation industry and related content industries have developed alongside the expansion of the domestic market, as the market for animated features has been sustained by domestic demands. Chapter 2 describes the overall shape and the characteristics of the spatial structure of the transactional relationships among studios in Tokyo and the characteristics of the labor market, which may have influenced the process of industrial agglomeration.

Chapter 3 describes the South Korean animation industry and its development through subcontracting from Japanese and Western animation industries. In South Korea, the animation industry has agglomerated in the capital city, Seoul. There are both similarities and differences between the agglomeration structure of the industry in South Korea and that in Japan, the client country. This case study sheds light on how the following three factors influence agglomeration in the animation industry: the international division of labor, the transactional relationships between clients and subcontractors, and the labor market.

Chapter 4 describes the Chinese animation industry, which began to attract attention from the Japanese and Western animation industries in the 1990s. Although China is a subcontracted country of Japan and Western animation industries, as is South Korea, and its local industry has likewise developed under the influence of an international division of labor, the circumstances surrounding the Chinese industry are not the same. A description and analysis of the structure and the overall shape of the animation industry in the Shanghai region reveals the characteristics of its industrial agglomeration, which are different from those of the South Korean animation industry.

Chapters 5 and 6 will examine in greater depth the different viewpoints outlined in the previous chapters. The discussion will focus on the working styles at various studios and related facilities and present theories about the cooperation and creativity generated within these studios. At first glance, this might seem like a strange approach for a study on the agglomeration of the animation industry; however, because workers are the creative core of the metropolis, research on how they behave in the industry can provide revealing information about the animation industry. Chapter 5 focuses on the environments and activities of end workers in the animation industry in Tokyo along with the correlation between the spatial functions of their studios and creativity.

Although most animation studios are located and agglomerated in metropolises, some studios have established subsidiaries in local cities in Japan because of changes in the home and subcontracted countries. Political support is a crucial and essential form of investment for establishing studios or facilities in local cities; for example, a case study of Okinawa, Japan is also discussed. The rationality of the studios' strategy to secure subsidiaries in local cities in Japan is defended on the basis of these data. Chapter 6 also stresses the importance of communication between studios and the possibility of industrial promotion in the animation industry on the basis of data from fieldwork.

The last Chap. 7 will compare the agglomerated structures described in previous chapters to show how generality and regionality stimulate agglomeration. The derived structure reveals the factors behind the heterogeneous agglomeration of content industries and cultural industries, the leading industries in metropolises.

References

Abrahamson M (2004) Global cities. Oxford University Press, New York

Arai Y, Nakamura H, Sato H, Nakazawa T, Sugizaki K (2004) Multimedia and internet business clusters in central Tokyo. Urban Geogr 25:483–500. doi:10.2747/0272-3638.25.5.483

Bain AL (2004) Female artistic identity in place: the studio. Social Cult Geogr 5:171–193. doi:10.1080/14649360410001690204

Bain AL (2005) Constructing an artistic identity. Work Employ Soc 9:25–46. doi:10.1177/0950017005051280

Blair H (2003) Winning and losing in flexible labour markets: the formation and operation of networks of interdependence in the UK film industry. Sociology 37:677–694. doi:10.1177/00380385030374003

Camagni R (1991) Introduction: from the local 'milieu' to innovation through cooperation networks. In: Camagni R (ed) Innovation networks: spatial perspective. Belhaven Press, London

Capello R (1999) Spatial transfer of knowledge in high technology Milieux: learning versus collective learning processes. Reg Stud 33:353–365. doi:10.1080/00343409950081211

Clark TN (2003) Urban amenities: lakes, opera, and juice bars: do they drive development? In: Clark TN (ed) The city as an entertainment machine. Elsevier, Oxford

Coe NM (2000) The view from out west: embeddedness, inter-personal relations and the development of an indigenous film industry in Vancouver. Geoforum 31:391–407. doi:10.1016/S0016-7185(00)00005-1

Coe NM (2001) A hybrid agglomeration? The development of a satellite-marshallian industrial district in Vancouver's film industry. Urban Stud 38:1753–1775. doi:10.1080/00420980120084840

Crang P (1997) Cultural turns and the (re) constitution of economic geography. In: Lee R, Wills J (eds) Geography of economies. Arnold, New York

Development and Reform Center for China's State Administration of Radio, Film and Television (2006) 2006nian Zhongguo Guangbo Dianying Dianshi Fazhan Baogao [Report on development of China's radio, film and television 2006]. Social Sciences Academic Press, Beijing (Chinese)

Drake G (2003) 'This place gives me space': place and creativity in the creative industries. Geoforum 34:511–524. doi:10.1016/S0016-7185(03)00029-0

Editorial Board of China Animation Yearbook (2007) Zhongguo Donghua Nianjian 2006 [Yearbook of Chinese animation 2006]. China Radio and TV Press, Beijing (Chinese)

Elmer G, Gasher M (2005) Contracting out Hollywood: runaway productions and foreign location shooting. Rowman & Littlefield Publishers, Lanham

Florida R (1995) Toward the learning region. Futures 27:527–536. doi:10.1016/0016-3287(95)00021-n

Florida R (2002) The rise of the creative class. Basic Books, New York

Florida R (2005) The flight of the creative class. Collins, New York

Florida R (2008) Who's your city? Basic Books, New York

Friedman TL (2007) The world is flat, 3rd edn. Picador, New York

Furukawa S (2010) Kurieita no Shuseki ni okeru Nettowaku Kozo: Osakashi Kitaku Ogimachi Sheuhen o Jirei ni [The creators' network in the metropolitan agglomeration: a case study of Ogimachi area in Osaka city]. Ann Jpn Assoc Econ Geogr 56:88–105 (Japanese)

Gibson C, Murphy P, Freeston R (2002) Employment and socio-spatial relations in Australia's cultural economy. Aust Geogr 33:173–189. doi:10.1080/00049180220150990

Goldsmith B, O'Regan T, Australian Film Commission and Australian Key Centre for Cultural and Media Policy and Creative Industries Research and Applications Centre (2003) Cinema cities, media cities: the contemporary international studio complex. Australian Film Commission, Sydney

Govil N (2005) Hollywood's effects, Bollywood FX. In: Elmer G, Gasher M (eds) Contracting out Hollywood: runaway productions and foreign location. Rowman & Littlefield, Oxford

Han C (2005) Dijital Aenimeisyeon Jejak Paipelain eu Sisutem Jeokhabhwa e kwanhan Yeongoo [A study on the system adapting process of production pipeline in digital animation]. Doctoral thesis, Sogang University (Korean)

Hanzawa S (2001) Tokyo ni okeru Animeshon Sangyo Shuseki no Kozo to Henyo [The structure and developing changes in the animation industry agglomeration in Tokyo]. Ann Jpn Assoc Ecno Geogr 47:288–302

Hanzawa S (2005) Kateiyo Bideo Gemu Sangyo no Bungyo Keitai to Chiriteki Tokusei [Characteristics of the Division of Labor and Geography in the Japanese Home Video Game Industry]. Geogr Rev Jpn 78:607–633

Hara S (2005) Gurobaru Kyoso Jidai ni okeru Nihon no Dejitaru Kontentsu Sangyo Shuseki no Kyoso Yuisei to Inobeshon no Hokosei: SD Gandamu Fosu Purojekuto o Jirei ni [Competitive advantage and innovation of digital content industrial clusters in Japan in global competition era: a case of "SD GUNDAMFORCE" project]. Ann Jpn Assoc Econ Geogr 51:368–386 (Japanese)

Hesmondhalgh D (2007) The cultural industries, 2nd edn. Sage, London

Hesmondhalgh D, Baker S (2011) Creative labour: media work in three cultural industries. Routledge, New York

Howkins J (2007) The creative economy, revised edn. Penguin Books, New York

Keeble D, Lawson C, Moore B, Wilkinson F (1999) Collective learning processes, networking and 'institutional thickness' in the Cambridge region. Reg Stud 33:319–332. doi:10.1080/713693557

Kim H (2001) Gooknae Aenimeisyeon ui Giheok Jejak Sisutem Modele kwanhan Yeongoo (The study of animation planning and production in Korea). The Report of the Korean Film Council 2001–9:30–38 (Korean)

Kong L, O'Connor J (2009) Creative economies, creative cities. Springer, New York

Korea Creative Content Agency (2010) 2010 Aenimeisyeon Saneop Baekseo [Animation industry white paper 2004]. Korea Creative Content Agency, Seoul (Korean)

Korea Culture & Contents Agency (2004) Daehanmingook Aenimeisyeon Saneop Baekseo [Korea animation industry white paper 2004]. Korea Culture & Contents Agency, Seoul (Korean)

Lent JA (1998) The animation industry and its offshore factories. In: Sussman G, Lent JA (eds) Global productions. Hampton Press, Cresskill

Lu H (2011) 2010 nian Zhongguo Donghua Dianshipian Fazhan Baogao [Report on development of China's animated television series in 2010]. In: Lu B, Zheng Y, Niu X (eds) Zhongguo Dongman Chanye Fazhan Baogao [Report on China animation industry]. Social Sciences Academic Press, Beijing (Chinese)

Lu B, Zheng Y, Niu X (2011) Tochoujiangu, Duoguanqixia, Shixian cong Donghua Daguo Dao Dongman Qiangguo de Kuayue [Taking overall consideration and multi-pronged approach to realize leap forward from a big animation country to a powerful animation country]. In: Lu B, Zheng Y, Niu X (eds) Zhongguo Dongman Chanye Fazhan Baogao [Report on China animation industry]. Social Sciences Academic Press, Beijing (Chinese)

Marksen A (1996) Sticky places in slippery space: a typology of industrial districts. Econ Geogr 72:293–313. doi:10.1080/713693557

Masubuchi T (2005) Indizu Ongaku Sangyo no Sozo Genba: Kokunai Chiiki deno Sangyoka no Kanosei [The creative place of Japanese independent music industry: the feasibility of industrialize on local regions]. Cult Econ 4:19–29. doi:10.11195/jace1998.4.3_19 (Japanese)

Masubuchi T (2007) Kontentsu Sangyo to shiteno Hoso Media Chiiki Senryaku: Sozo Toshiron o Haikei ni [The regional strategy of broadcast media as one of the content industry: in the context of the creative city theory]

Miller T, Leger MC (2001) Runaway production, runaway consumption, runaway citizenship: the new international division of cultural labor. Emergen 11:89–115. doi:10.1080/10457220120044684

Ministry of Economy, Trade and Industry (2008) Gijutsu Senryaku Mappu 2008 (Kontentsu Sangyo Bunya) [the technological strategy map 2008 (content industry sector)]. Ministry of Economy, Trade and Industry Web site. http://www.meti.go.jp/policy/mono_info_service/contents/downloadfiles/gizyutumap.pdf. Accessed 30 Dec 2011 (Japanese)

Ministry of Economy, Trade and Industry (2011) Kontentsu Sangyo no Genjo to Kongo no Hatten no Hokosei [a Present Condition and Perspectives of future development in Contents Industry]. Ministry of Economy, Trade and Industry Web site. http://www.meti.go.jp/policy/mono_info_service/contents/downloadfiles/genjou_hatten.pdf. Accessed 30 Dec 2011 (Japanese)

Piore MJ, Sable CF (1984) The second industrial divide: possibilities for prosperity, Reprintth edn. Basic Books, New York

Porter ME (2008) On competition: updated and expanded edition. Harvard Business Review Press, Boston

Power D (2002) "Cultural industries" in Sweden: an assessment of their place in the Swedish economy. Econ Geogr 78:103–127. doi:10.1111/j.1944-8287.2002.tb00180.x

Power D, Scott AJ (eds) (2004) Cultural industries and the production of culture. Routledge, New York

Pratt AC (1997) The cultural industries production system: a case study of employment change in Britain, 1984–91. Environ Plan A 29:1953–1974. doi:10.1068/a291953

Qin X (2006) Zhongguo Donghuapian de Chanye Jingjixue Yanjiu [The economics of China's animation industry]. China Market Press, Beijing (Chinese)

Saxenian A (1994) Regional advantage: culture and competition in silicon valley and route 128. Harvard University Press, Massachusetts

Saxenian A (2006) The new argonauts. Harvard University Press, Massachusetts

Scott AJ (1988a) Territorial reproduction and transformation in a local labor market: the animated film workers of Los Angeles. In: Metropolis. The University of California Press, California

Scott AJ (1988b) Flexible production systems and regional development. Int J Urban Reg Res 12:171–186. doi:10.1111/j.1468-2427.1988.tb00448.x

Scott AJ (2000) The cultural economy of cities. Sage, London

Scott AJ (2004) Cultural-products industries and urban economic development: prospects for growth and market contestation in global context. Urban Aff Rev 39:461–490. doi:10.1177/1078087403261256

Scott AJ, Pope NE (2007) Hollywood, Vancouver, and the world: employment relocation and the emergence of satellite production centers in the motion-picture industry. Environ Plan A 39:1364–1381. doi:10.1068/a38215

Shin B (2002) Aenimeisyeon Saneop eu Nodongkwajeong e kwanhan Tamsaekjeok Yeongoo [An exploratory study on the production processes of animation industry]. Korean J Labor Stud 8:111–142 (Korean)

Throsby D (2001) Economics and culture. Cambridge University Press, New York

Vinodrai T (2006) Reproducing Toronto's design ecology: career paths, intermediaries, and local labor markets. Econ Geogr 83:237–263. doi:10.1111/j.1944-8287.2006.tb00310.x

Yamamoto K (2007) Tokyo ni okeru Animeshon Sangyo no Shuseki Mekanizumu: Kigyokan Torihiki to Rodosijyo ni Chakumoku shite [Agglomeration mechanism of the animation industry in Tokyo: focus on business-to-business transactions and the labor market]. Geogr Rev Jpn 80:442–458 (Japanese)

Yamamoto K (2008) Souru ni okeru Animeshon Sangyo no Shuseki to Tokushitsu: Kokusai Bungyo oyobi Rodo Shijo ni Chakumoku shite [Agglomeration and the characteristics of the animation industry in Seoul: focus on international division of labor and the labor market]. Quart J Geogr 60:185–206 (Japanese). http://dx.doi.org/10.5190/tga.60.185

Yamamoto K (2009) Shanhai Chiiki ni okeru Animeshon Sangyo no Shuseki Kozo: Kaigai Izongata Kigyo no Jirei o Chushin ni [Agglomeration of the animation industry in the Shanghai region, China: special reference to firms based on overseas transaction]. Geogr Sci 64:228–249 (Japanese)

You J, Cha T (2004) 3D Aenimeisyeon Sangeop eisseoseo Munjejeom kwa Baljeon Banghyang e kwanhan Yeongoo [A study on proposition and future perspectives in 3D animation industry]. Jeongbodijainyeongoo (Inform Des Stud) 7:111–120 (Korea)

Chapter 2
Agglomeration of the Animation Industry in Tokyo, Japan

Abstract The agglomeration structure of the animation industry in Tokyo is described in terms of the characteristics of the transactional relationships among studios and in the labor market. Animation studios are concentrated in the western suburbs of Tokyo. Some studios receive orders from major clients such as related content firms located in the central business district of Tokyo and continue to distribute their work to others in the industry. Transactions among studios are conducted with short delivery times. Some parts of lower processes such as animation picture and coloring process are outsourced to foreign studios. Studios conduct transactions with each other for complementary labor and techniques. Workers acquire skills and obtain work through personal connections within and outside their studios to avoid income instability. Although the technical schools where they learn basic animation techniques are located across the country, skilled workers later gravitate to the animation industry in Tokyo because the city offers many opportunities to find work.

Keywords Domestic market • Personal connections • Technical schools • Tokyo • Transactional relationships

2.1 Introduction

Since 1960, the development of the Japanese animation industry has kept pace with national demand, with most animation studios located in Tokyo. For this reason, clarifying the agglomeration structure of the region's animation industry and the extent of its development is essential to understanding agglomeration as a general process in metropolises.

The research method involved a questionnaire survey administered to workers at animation production studios located in Tokyo and interviews with studio managers. In May 2005, questionnaires were mailed to a sample of 278 studios chosen from telephone directories. Data obtained through these questionnaires were

© Springer Japan 2014

K. Yamamoto, *The Agglomeration of the Animation Industry in East Asia*,
International Perspectives in Geography: AJG Library 4,
DOI 10.1007/978-4-431-55093-8_2

extracted to analyze the characteristics of each studio's location as discussed in a later section in this chapter. Overall, 48 studios (17.3 %) responded with valid answers. The questionnaire consisted of items assessing basic attributes, major business fields, major clients, and important transaction factors. Individual worker questionnaires were administered in November 2005 at one of the studios that had replied to the initial survey, and 20 freelancers were interviewed. The worker questionnaire consisted of items assessing monthly income, opportunities for skill learning, and the number of projects completed in a month. Over this time period, manager interviews were conducted at 12 studios, with 10 managers responding face-to-face, one over the phone, and one by email. The current study is based on these data and their analysis.

2.2 Growth in the Japanese Animation Industry

2.2.1 Japanese Animation Market Structure

Figure 2.1 shows the total sales of the Japanese animation industry, as reported in the "Anime sangyo repoto 2012" (Report on the animation industry 2012) by the Association of Japanese Animations. Annual sales in 2011 are estimated to have been about 158.1 billion yen. Broadcast content constitutes the largest share of sales at 56.0 billion yen (35.4 %). The second largest share is merchandising sales at 24.4 billion yen (15.4 %). Despite the wide belief that Japanese animation is highly popular with overseas consumers, sales from the overseas market totaled only 16.0 billion yen (10.1 %).

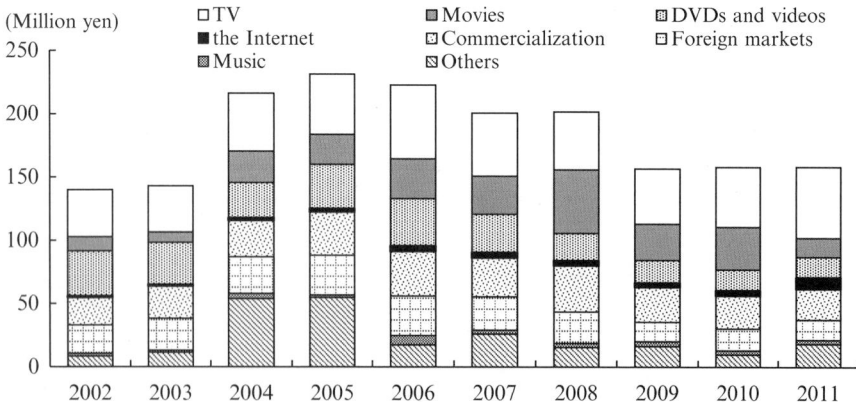

Fig. 2.1 Net sales by fields in the Japanese Animation Industry (2002–2011). *Note*: This graph is a narrow interpretation of the animation market by the Association of Japanese Animations (2012). The name and product field of each type of media have been modified to reflect those of Fig. 2.2. "Others" after 2008 include "entertainment." *Source*: Based on "Anime Sangyo Repoto 2012" (a report on the animation industry 2012) by the Association of Japanese Animations, p. 53

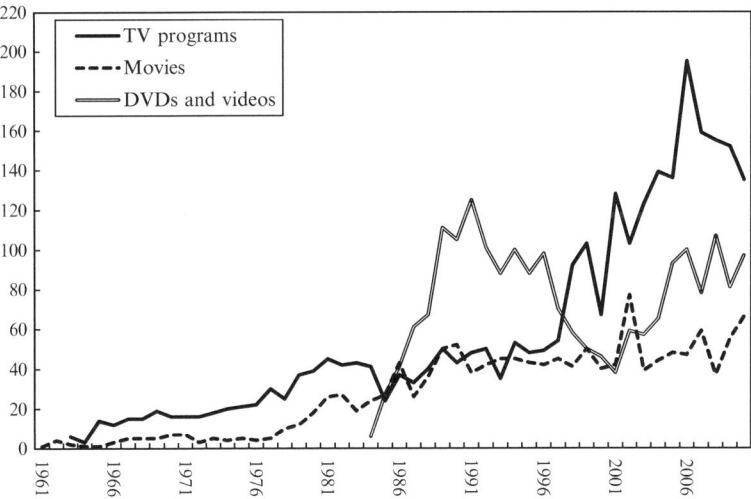

Fig. 2.2 Number of animated features newly broadcast via TV, movies, and Video/DVD. *Note*: The number of newly broadcast animated TV series is based on data provided by the Association of Japanese Animations (2012). Because of differences in the summarizing method and the references, this figure is different from that in Yamamoto (2012a). *Source*: Based on Yamamoto (2012a) Fig. 1, "Animage" Vol. 405, "Anime Sangyo Repoto 2012" (a report on the animation industry 2012) by the Association of Japanese Animations, p. 55

Figure 2.2 shows the changes in the number of annual series broadcasts as the animation industry developed rapidly through the late 1990s. The Japanese TV broadcasting market is now the main market for Japanese animation. Figure 2.3 illustrates the changes in the number of animated TV programs being shown in several timeslots in 1997, 2002, 2007, and 2012. This figure shows that the number of animated programs being broadcast during the midnight timeslot (after 11 p.m.) increased rapidly throughout the decade. These late-night animated shows are a basic product of the strategy to capture the main source of revenue from DVD and video sales to animation fans. According to Sudo (2008), this business practice was established in the mid-1990s and the market has expanded because of the increase in the number of Japanese animated programs for broadcast TV.

2.2.2 Japanese Animation Production Process and Introduction of Digital Technology

Workers in the animation industry can be roughly classified into the following three departments: the creative department, which handles the preproduction phase (planning, script, character design, storyboard, and layout); the production department, which handles the production and postproduction phase (key picture, animation picture, coloring, background, sound effects, shooting, special effects, and editing);

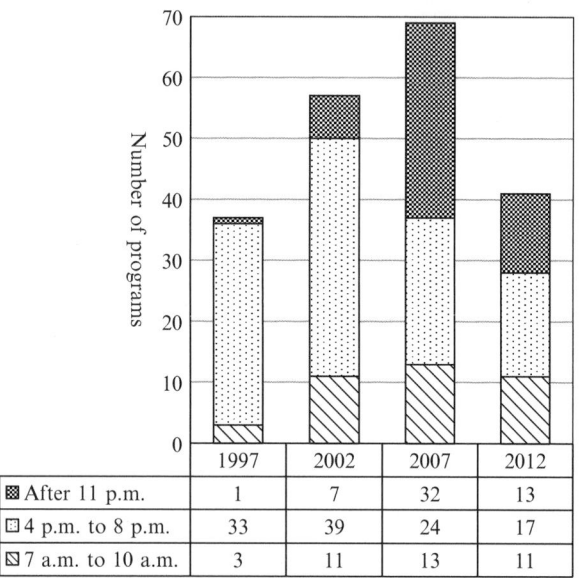

	1997	2002	2007	2012
▨ After 11 p.m.	1	7	32	13
▢ 4 p.m. to 8 p.m.	33	39	24	17
◪ 7 a.m. to 10 a.m.	3	11	13	11

Fig. 2.3 Number of TV animation programs by Timeslot in February 1997, 2002, 2007, and 2012. *Note*: The timeslot category is based on the definition by the Association of Japanese Animations. Animations broadcast during timeslots other than these three were excluded. *Source*: Based on "Animage" (Vol. 225, 285, 345, 405)

and the directing department (project management and direction). The division of labor is more advanced in the production department than in the other two departments (Fig. 2.4).[1]

Although the recent advent of digitization in the animation industry has brought a kind of diversification to the production process, the degree to which digital technology has been implemented varies from one process to the next. According to a study by Hara (2005), all production processes after coloring have already been digitalized during the 2D animation (celluloid animation) stage of production. In the background process, both analog and digital drawing are used, but the analog method, i.e., paper and pencil, is popular in the key picture and animation picture stages (Fig. 2.5). As we learned in our interviews, inanimate objects are easy to draw using 3D computer graphics, but 3D computer graphics are not suitable for depicting subtle emotions on human or animal faces; hence, the use of 3D computer graphics for the animation of organic objects is restricted to only part of the whole process.[2]

---

[1] Layout and special effects are sometimes classified as production and postproduction, respectively.

[2] Before the advent of digitization, it took workers several years to learn the techniques required for the coloring process. Thanks to the popularization of computer-assisted drawing, this learning period has been shortened to 2 or 3 months because digital coloring does not require animators to possess the precision and discernment levels required for key picture work, animation picture work, and celluloid coloring. For example, workers in the coloring process cannot accidentally color off the edge of a painting or color unevenly when using digital coloring on the computer, and the operation of coloring software is the first important technique learned by workers in the coloring process. On the other hand, supervisors in key picture and animation picture departments demand that animators depict their visions accurately, which is a process that is hard to learn.

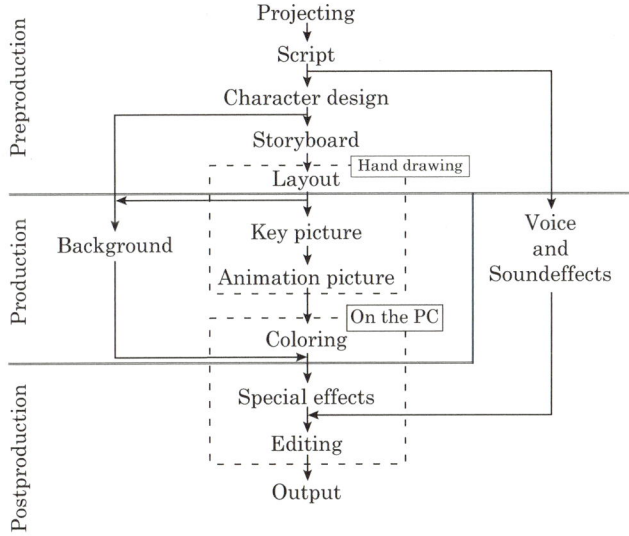

Fig. 2.4 Japanese animation production process

Fig. 2.5 Animation picture department workspace (2006). *Note*: Each image in an animated program is drawn by hand, even today

Washiya (2004) showed that it requires 2 months for 150 workers to produce the 3,000 hand-drawn pictures that make up 25 min of animation, whereas the animation picture and coloring processes—the lower processes of animation production—can be sustained by 30–40 workers each. The animation picture and coloring phases of production are very labor-intensive processes that are handled one after another, meaning that the first process has to be completed before the second process can begin. In addition, these two lower processes often need to absorb delays in the schedule that are created by the upper processes such as storyboard and layout (see Chap. 5, Fig. 5.1).

In Japan, over 130 new animated TV series are broadcast each year, and the animation industry is active year-round. Because a single animation studio cannot create all the necessary drawings for a complete series (which consists of multiple episodes), some episodes are outsourced to other studios. A single animated series may be produced by five or six gross-orderd[3] groups, each handling different episodes that air in rotation.

2.2.3   Location of Animation Studios in Tokyo

In the 1960s, TV animation was the leading content of the Japanese animation industry. Yamaguchi (2004) indicated that the producers of TV animation in the early years were workers in the film industry or cartoon writers. Prominent among these was Osamu Tezuka, who is well-known as the creator of Astro Boy. Other cartoon writers and animation studios congregated around his studio because of geographical proximity. Konagaya and Tomizawa (1999) indicate that another factor encouraging industrial agglomeration in this early phase was the locations of famous cartoon writers' residences or film studios. The parental animation studios, as well as their spinoff and satellite studios, were located close to film studios to obtain convenient access to shooting facilities rather than their prime contract industry. The film and comic industries were the precursors to the animation industry. As a result, animation studios and the industry as a whole have agglomerated in the western suburbs of Tokyo, where they remain to this day. This agglomeration began in the earliest stages of industrialization and has continued to develop up to the present day; as of 2014, 78.8 % (278 studios) of all animation studios were located within Tokyo, 37 % (105 studios) of which were concentrated in Nerima and Suginami wards (Fig. 2.6).

---

[3] A gross order is an order of work for multiple episodes of an animation series from the primary contractors. Subcontracted studios handle all of the production processes for the ordered episodes by themselves.

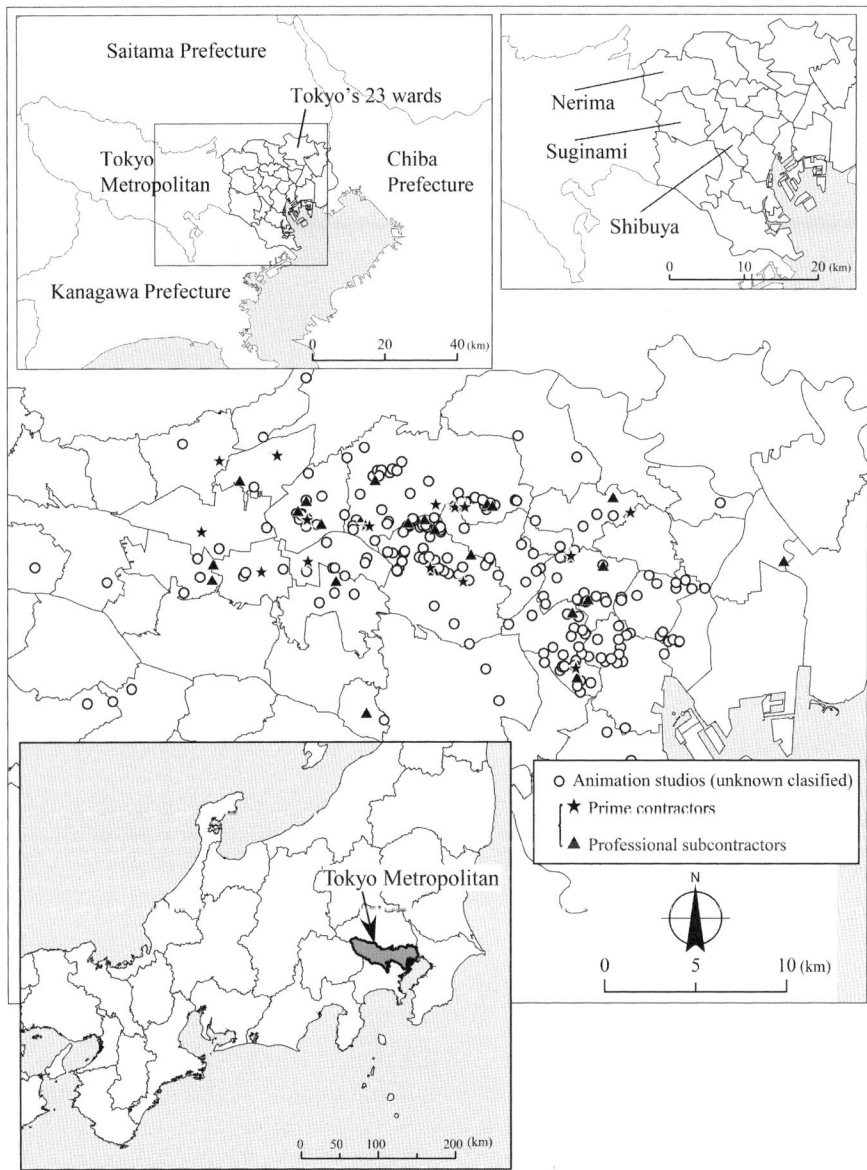

Fig. 2.6 Location of animation studios in Tokyo. *Source*: Questionnaire survey and field survey

2.3   Transaction Characteristics

2.3.1   Basic Studio Attributes

Animation studios are generally small. Forty out of 47 (81.5 %) studios possess less than 100 million yen[4] in capital, and 26 of these have less than ten million yen. Only 16 out of 41 (39.2 %) studios have annual sales between 100 and 300 million yen, whereas 14 (34.1 %) studios have annual sales less than 100 million yen. In addition, 17 out of 45 (37.4 %) studios employ fewer than 20 regular workers.[5]

The larger studios tend to contract with firms in other industries or to diversify their business beyond animation production. As a result, their dependence on their animation production departments is lower than those of smaller studios. It is not the size of the studio, but the types of transactions it can make, which defines its role in the production process. Animation studios are classified into two types according to their trading practices. The first type is the "primary contractor" studios, which manage whole projects by keeping all of the production in-house. They receive orders from clients and produce animated TV series by themselves or by outsourcing work to secondary contractors. The other type is the "professional subcontractor" studios, which take on specific production processes from primary contractors and then deliver half-finished products to the primary contractors who then complete the projects.

The results of our questionnaire show that 18 of the studios in the present study are "primary contractors" while 26 are "professional subcontractors." Two studios identified themselves as "others" and another two answered "unspecified." Some primary contractor studios also take on specialized subcontracts to maintain a stable business income. Likewise, some professional subcontractor studios outsource certain jobs, such as the planning of an animation product series or video software production, as subsidiary business.[6]

2.3.2   Structure and Spatial Pattern of Transactions

The studios were requested to answer additional questions regarding their two clients with the largest sales transactions by describing these clients in terms of studio type and location as well as the proportion of their own total sales that comes from these two clients, the ordering process, and the use of transactional contracts or lack

---

[4] 100 yen = 0.75 US dollars as of May 1, 2005.

[5] A few of the studios did not answer some of our questions. As a result, the numbers of answers are different.

[6] The major focus of our 25 subcontractors is animation production (100 %). Their secondary activities include animation projecting (44.0 %), the production of video software (32.0 %), movie production (28.0 %), and commercial message production (24.0 %).

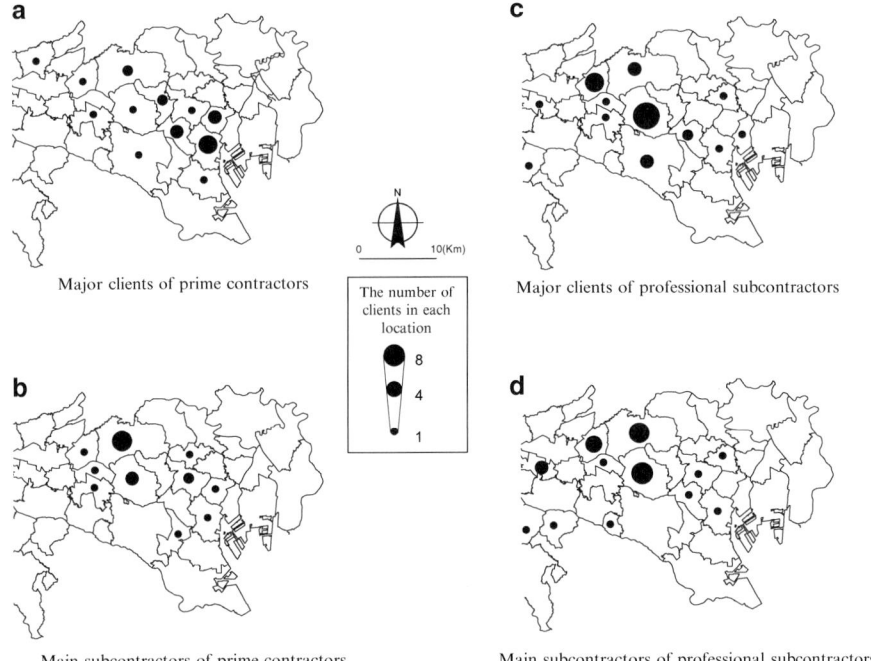

Fig. 2.7 Spatial Distribution Patterns of Animation Studios' Clients. *Source*: Questionnaire survey

thereof. Figure 2.7 maps these transactions as of 2004. In this section, the structure and spatial pattern of these transactions are elaborated on the basis of the studios' answers and Fig. 2.7.

2.3.2.1   Receiving Orders

Primary contractors have 8.5 clients on average, and only two studios have over 20 clients. Of the 16 (81.3 %) major clients, 13 were in the animation industry. This result supports the hypothesis that some primary contractors, as previously noted, specialize in receiving "gross orders," which they subcontract out to stabilize their income. The remaining clients are in fields other than the animation and content industries, such as publishing (31.3 %), video game development (18.8 %), film-making (12.5 %), broadcasting (12.5 %), and others that are not as well represented. According to the results of our interviews, these contractors meet weekly with any sponsors when they are working on an animated TV series. The persons in charge of the studios and those in charge of TV production attend these meetings where they discuss production strategies and adjust their animation projects to coincide with the sponsors' marketing strategies. The large proportion of total order volume that comes from each studio's two main clients suggests that many studios are heavily dependent on their top clients; in fact, eight out of 13 primary contractors receive over half of their entire order volume from a single top client.

Professional subcontractors tend to have more clients than primary contractors do, with 12.3 on average. Six of our professional subcontractors have over 20 clients, and one studio has 45 clients, which is a very large number in the animation industry. Although these subcontractors receive orders from various clients, 91.7 % of their major clients are in the same industry; this percentage is higher for subcontractors than for primary contractors. Regarding proportions of order volume from top clients, only nine out of 23 studios are dependent on their single biggest client for more than half of their whole order volume. These results show that professional subcontractors have many clients and sustain primary contractors with their flexibility.

2.3.2.2 Subcontracting

Primary contractors typically have more subcontractors than clients; one studio even had more than 100 subcontractors. Most of these subcontractor studios are in the animation industry (94.1 %), while others are primarily in movie production, music production, or multimedia-related services. However, most professional subcontractors have fewer than ten subcontractors, 95.5 % of which were in the same industry.

Tokyo is home to 96.8 % (123 out of the 127 studios) of the major clients and subcontractors described in this part of the survey. Figure 2.7 shows the pattern of major clients' and subcontractors' localization in Tokyo. Panel (a) shows the major clients of primary contractors. The number of orders from related content industries, such as publishing, broadcasting services, and video game development, is relatively high, and the distribution of these related content industries is concentrated in the Tokyo central business district (CBD), such as Minato and Chiyoda wards (e.g., Arai et al. 2004). This distribution supports the fact that primary contractors have clients in related content industries. Panel (b) shows the major subcontractors of primary contractors. Their distribution is concentrated in Suginami and Nerima wards where animation production studios agglomerate. Panels (c) and (d) show the major clients and subcontractors of professional subcontractors. Distribution of these is highly concentrated in Suginami Ward, Nerima Ward, and Nishitokyo City, where studios from the same industry have accumulated (see Fig. 2.6) because of the powerful influence of transactions in the industry. In other words, primary contractors obtain work from related content industries, then distribute individual tasks within each project to others in the industry, while professional subcontractors take on and perform these jobs in the same industry.

2.3.3 Characteristics of Business Transactions

2.3.3.1 Important Factors to Consider in Business Relationships

Table 2.1 enumerates several important factors that studios consider when conducting business. Among studios that accepted subcontracts from other studios, "trust regarding payment" from the client is an important factor in deciding whether to accept a subcontract. Other major factors included "whether the work is in a field that the studio is good at," "whether the studio can handle the assigned workload," and "conventional business relationship." In the case of professional subcontractors, "geographical proximity" was also emphasized.

Table 2.1 Important factors in trade relationships

Items	Primary contractors	(%)	Professional subcontractors	(%)
Factors considered in accepting a subcontract				
Whether the work is in a field that the studio is good at	22	(71.0)	27	(58.7)
Trust regarding payment	20	(64.5)	29	(63.0)
Whether the studio can handle the assigned workload	12	(38.7)	24	(52.2)
Conventional business relationship	12	(38.7)	20	(43.5)
Viable delivery time	7	(22.6)	10	(21.7)
Having business relationships with the same capital studios	2	(6.5)	1	(2.2)
High pay rate	4	(12.9)	1	(2.2)
Favorable business conditions	1	(3.2)	7	(15.2)
Geographical proximity	0	(0.0)	6	(13.0)
Number of studios replying	31	–	41	–
Factors considered in subcontracting work out				
Shortage of in-house labor force	18	(60.0)	28	(70.0)
Complementary skills	14	(46.7)	7	(17.5)
Conventional business relationship	11	(36.7)	18	(45.0)
Trust regarding product quality	11	(36.7)	16	(40.0)
Short delivery time	10	(33.3)	21	(52.2)
Geographical proximity	7	(23.3)	10	(25.0)
Cheap labor force	1	(3.3)	4	(10.0)
High pay rate	1	(3.3)	1	(2.5)
Having business relationship with the same capital studios	0	(0.0)	1	(2.5)
Number of studios replying	30	–	40	–

Thirty primary contractors and 40 professional subcontractors replied with multiple answers
Source: Questionnaire survey

Among studios that subcontract some of the work they receive from clients, the most important factor in the decision to subcontract was whether there was "shortage of in-house labor force," which indicates a lack of complementary labor. "Complementary skills" was the second most commonly chosen item by primary contractors, though it was chosen less frequently by professional subcontractors. "Short delivery time" was the second most commonly chosen item by professional subcontractors. To summarize, in considering a business transaction, primary contractors emphasized complementary skills as well as complementary labor, while professional subcontractors put even more emphasis on complementary labor in the short term.

As common characteristics of transactions in the industry, studios emphasized "conventional business relationship." They also emphasized "trust regarding product quality" when ordering jobs and the area of specialty when receiving jobs. Technical competence was a major criterion in choosing partners.

2.3.3.2 Delivery Time

Table 2.2 shows the delivery times specified by clients in the animation industry. In the case of primary contractors, this table reveals that most delivery times were longer than 2 months. One reason for this is that most major clients are in related content industries, as shown by the distribution of the clients of the animation studios. The business they have in common is centered around TV programs, and the delivery times in these contracts are rather long, generally ranging from 2 to 13 months and sometimes longer. Another reason for the long delivery times is that these transactions represent gross orders for work that will be ongoing throughout the duration of the animated series.

In the case of professional subcontractors, on the other hand, only around 25 % of all studios reported requesting delivery times ranging from 2 to 6 months, while 73 % of them reported requesting very short delivery times like "1 day," "1 week,"

Table 2.2 Distribution of due dates for orders received

Lead times	Primary contractors	Professional subcontractors
1 day	0	9
1 week	1	12
10 days	0	7
1 month	2	5
2–3 months	13	7
4–6 months	8	4
7–9 months	3	0
10–12 months	4	1
Over 13 months	1	0
Number of studios replying	32	45

Source: Questionnaire survey

and "10 days." This distribution of delivery times arises from the fact that business transactions with medium-length delivery times tend to be for gross orders whereas those with short delivery times tend to be for work on only a small portion of the whole animated series, e.g., one or two episodes. Moreover, these short delivery times promote the need for geographical proximity among the participating animation production studios.

According to our interviews, schedule delays typically arise during the preproduction processes, such as the "storyboard" and "layout" stages, and are then absorbed during the lower processes, such as "key picture," "animation picture," and "coloring," through insistence on short delivery times, with deadlines as tight as 1 day. In addition, key pictures and animation pictures are still drawn with pencil and paper in Japan, although the digital technology that could replace this stage is available. These half-finished products are then delivered to the person in charge at the client studio. To make this delivery faster and easier, the animation studios prefer geographical proximity to mitigate time constraints in transactions between business partners (see Chap. 5 for more detailed information).

2.3.3.3 Contracts

We asked whether studios explicitly record contract details when conducting business. For studios placing orders, primary contractors recorded these details in 18 of 27 cases, while professional subcontractors recorded them in only eight of 46 cases. For studios receiving orders, 21 of 27 of the primary contractors and 31 of 35 of the professional subcontractors did not explicitly record details. It appears that these studios usually do not explicitly record contract details during transactions within the industry.

Based on our interviews, there are three main reasons why these studios do not explicitly record contract details. First, drafting documents leads to rigid contractual coverage, difficulties of industrial practices, additional services based on tacit understanding, and flexible and impromptu responses in the case of delays in the upper processes such as storyboard, layout and quality checking for key pictures and animation pictures (see Sect. 2.2.2 and Chap. 5 for more detailed information). Second, these documents guarantee the credibility of contractual execution and include compensation for any breach in exchange. Typically, animation studios are so small that any such penalty would severely affect their business conditions. Third, transactions between professional subcontractors are mainly based on horizontal relationships, in which there is a tacit understanding between the parties. Whether the products are of acceptable quality depends on the subjective judgment of the person in charge, and very short delivery times require studios to be flexible with regard to production. In other words, it is difficult to define an acceptable product condition in contract documents. Moreover, studios prefer the benefits that stem from an avoidance of documentation, which is based on accepted custom in the animation industry. Industrial organization theory is useful to interpret this characteristic transactional relationship. Williamson (1983) pointed out that transactions based on mutual trust within a peer group can tolerate a higher degree of risk than transactions in the market can. Implicit contracts and contract renegotiation should also be discussed in the context of the new institutional economics.[7] Players can save significant contract costs through relying on implicit contracts constrained by something held in common such as transaction customs. In addition, when contract details are not explicitly recorded, they can be renegotiated between the studios to maximize profits. Although these points have been discussed with regard to the employment relationships between the firms and their employees, they can also be applied to the transaction relationships between studios.

While primary contractors are the biggest clients of the subcontract studios, the biggest clients of the primary contractors are outside the industry, with delivery times usually between 2 months and 1 year. Given these circumstances, it is understandable that primary contractors and their clients prefer the credibility of contractual execution.

2.3.3.4 Characteristics of Conducting Business with Overseas Studios

Some of the primary contractors and subcontractors surveyed in this study conduct business with overseas studios. Nine examples of such relationships were reported in the survey, and 28 examples of transactions with animation production companies based in East Asia were reported; the major subcontracting countries, South Korea and China, were the locations in most cases. These transactions occurred with partners in South Korea (15 business transactions: 11 in Seoul and 4 unknown), China (seven business transactions: two each in Shanghai and Wuxi, one in Changzhou and two unknown), Indonesia (two business transactions; one each in Denpasar and Bandung), the United States (one in Los Angeles), and unspecified countries (three) (Table 2.3).[8]

In the case of business conducted with South Korean companies, the processes ordered mostly consisted of animation picture (nine transactions), coloring (eight transactions), and key picture (seven transactions). Other processes requested were background (five) and others (two). In the case of business with China, however, the main processes ordered were animation picture (seven) and coloring (seven), whereas the key picture process was ordered only once.

When asked to discuss their reasons for ordering work from South Korean studios, Japanese studios emphasized "shortage of in-house labor force" (nine transactions, 60.0 %), "complementary skills" (seven transactions, 46.7 %), and "short delivery time" (five, 33.3 %). Meanwhile, regarding work ordered from

---

[7] As a textbook for learners, Milgrom and Roberts (1992) would be appropriate.

[8] The overseas clients in these relationships were in South Korea (one business transaction), the United States (four business transactions), France (one business transaction), the United Kingdom (one business transaction), and unspecified countries (two business transactions). The industries of these clients included animation production (four), publishing (two), music production (one), toy manufacturing (one), and financing (one).

Table 2.3 Subcontracted animation processes by region

Process	Country/City									
	South Korea (15)		China (7)				Indonesia (2)		U.S. (1)	
	Seoul (11)	– (4)	Shanghai (2)	Wuxi (2)	Changzhou (1)	– (2)	DPS (1)	BDO (1)	LA (1)	– (3)
Production										1
Key picture	5	2			1					3
Animation picture	5	4	2	2	1	2				2
Coloring	4	4	2	2	1	2				1
Background	5						1	1		2
Editing	2								1	
–										

Source: Questionnaire survey

Numbers in parentheses after country and city names indicate the number of top clients of respondents in 2004

DPS Denpasar, *BDO* Bandung, *LA* Los Angeles; – unknown

China, Japanese studios emphasized "shortage of in-house labor force" (six transactions, 85.7 %), "cheap labor force" (five transactions, 71.4 %), and "short delivery time" (four, 57.1 %). These figures suggest that Japanese studios expect different advantages from outsourcing to South Korea and China. The processes ordered from Chinese studios are mainly labor-intensive and lower-level processes, such as animation picture and coloring, because of the significant difference made by a cheap labor force. From South Korean studios, however, better technique and product quality are expected (see Yamamoto (2012a) and Yamamoto (2012b) for more information).

Short delivery time was the most strongly emphasized condition with regard to both Japanese–South Korean transactions and Japanese–Chinese transactions, although short delivery time and overseas trade might initially seem incompatible. They can coexist, however, because Japanese studios have developed remarkable logistics to support their transactions with the other two countries. First, some studios use professional delivery systems for transportation between Japan and the other two countries. Second, materials can be transported by association delivery, perhaps through an association founded by several animation studios.[9] The transportation days for those deliveries are different from each other but are adjusted to cover every day.[10] In association deliveries, the person in charge from one studio in the association flies to South Korea and China to collect the products being sent to all of the studios[11] (Figs. 2.8 and 2.9). The persons in charge of the South Korean and Chinese studios await the arrival of the persons in charge of the Japanese studios at the airport and deliver all of their products to the association at once. Representatives from the South Korean or Chinese studios can also visit the Japanese studios commissioning the work to receive products and deliver finished work to the person in charge. This mutually cooperative system enables South Korean and Chinese studios to deliver their work within a short timeframe.[12]

---

[9] As of 2007, one professional delivery system and three association delivery systems were in place between Japan and South Korea, and one association delivery system was in place between Japan and China. Eleven Japanese studios and 12 South Korean studios participated in an association delivery system. The author accompanied an animation producer on the association delivery that transported approximately 100 kg of products consisting mainly of work on paper, such as storyboards, layouts, key pictures, and animation pictures (Fig. 2.9).

[10] According to our interviews, the time and effort required for transportation is not significantly greater in transactions with South Korean or Chinese studios than in those with studios in smaller Japanese cities. Because the cost of labor is cheaper in South Korea and China than in Japan, a division of labor between Japan and South Korea or China is a practical choice.

[11] Japanese animation studios use Narita International Airport for their association deliveries because of its departure times. The interviews showed that production activity all through the night is common and that instantaneous production is emphasized in the industry (see Chap. 5 for more detailed information). For this reason, early morning transportation by car is suitable because of the reduced frequency of traffic jams and the ease by which schedules can be managed, thereby saving time. Pickup times are set between 5:00 a.m. to 6:30 a.m., and Narita International Airport offers morning flights, reducing transportation time to a minimum.

[12] During an association delivery round trip, the person in charge from Japan stays and supervises operations at the South Korean or Chinese partner studios.

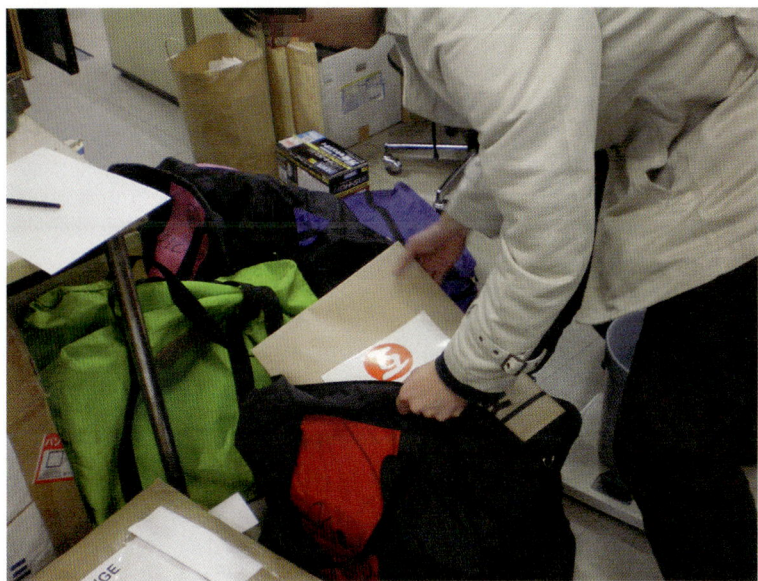

Fig. 2.8 Packing a half-finished product for Association delivery. *Note*: Duty studios in Japan receive half-finished products from midnight to early morning. *Source*: Based on Yamamoto (2012b) Photo 6-2

Fig. 2.9 Association delivery at Incheon International Airport. *Note*: A representative of the duty studio in Japan transports the package by commercial airline. *Source*: Based on Yamamoto (2012b) Photo 6-3

2.4   Characteristics of the Labor Market: Freelancers

According to our questionnaire results, the total number of freelancers participating in our study was 1,391 compared with 898 regular workers. However, the number of freelancers was based on figures reported by the studios, and the data might have been counted twice. At one studio, freelancers account for more than 90 % of its workers. Based on these facts, it is clear that a large number of freelancers is characteristic of the labor market in the animation industry.

Table 2.4 shows the distribution of regular employees and freelancers by job field. There are many regular employees in the directing department, such as "directors" (208 out of 227 workers), while most freelancers are in creative and manufacturing departments, especially "rendering" (175 out of the 683 workers), "key picture" (517 workers), and "animation picture" (324 workers). This association between employment type and job type is because of certain distinct characteristics of the jobs. "Directors" are responsible for management and business, and it is necessary for studios to employ regular workers in this regard for management stability. On the other hand, in fields like "rendering," "key picture," and "animation picture," although studios require a number of suitable workers skilled in each area, the expense of keeping all those workers permanently employed would be tremendous.

Table 2.4 Number of workers by job type and job field

Job fields	Regulars	Freelancers
Producer	44	44
Director	208	19
Rendering	77	175
Key picture	166	517
Animation picture	120	324
Coloring	126	184
Background	130	58
Shooting	136	31
Sound	4	9
Editing	20	11
3D computer graphic	28	19
Other	36	0
Total	1,099	1,391

Source: Questionnaire survey
The number of regulars is the total number of workers regardless of whether they serve concurrently

"Key picture" and "animation picture," in particular, require intensive labor and thus are unsuited to permanent employment.[13]

2.4.1   Supply System of the Labor Force

Conditions that determine whether employees are permanent or freelance are often related to their job backgrounds. This section focuses on the entry courses taken by workers, the reasons why studios hire regular workers, and the use of technical schools as a resource for developing labor skills.

Based on our survey data regarding entry courses and the final educational backgrounds of regular workers, it appears that 28 out of the 48 studios (58.3 %) mainly employ new graduates, while 17 out of the 48 studios (35.4 %) mainly employ experienced workers. Specifically, 23 out of the 48 studios (47.9 %) answered that their experienced workers came from the "animation industry," while 29 out of the 48 studios (60.4 %) answered that most of their employees have a final educational background in a "technical school of animation." A few workers came from related content industries, such as film (one studio), publishing (one studio), and video game development (one studio). Consequently, the main sources of regular employees are graduates from technical schools and experienced workers transferring within the industry.

As Table 2.5 shows, 35 out of the 48 studios emphasized "positive attitude toward work" as the most important criterion for employing regular workers. Other important criteria were "communication skills," "cooperation to work in a team," "skills above a specific level," "rich creativity," and "adaptation to the severe working environment." The studios emphasize not only the employees' techniques, but also their specialties and endurance.

An examination of the results from the questionnaire for freelancers shows that the freelancers consisted of one producer, four directors, four rendering specialists, eight key picture specialists, and three coloring specialists.

The remaining positions held by freelancers were "student" (13 respondents), "animation production" (four respondents), "film making" (one respondent), "others" (one respondent), and one nonrespondent. This result demonstrates that most freelancers enter the industry with no experience in other industries after graduating from a technical school. Freelancers' final academic backgrounds were "technical school" (14 respondents), "high school" (three respondents), "university" (three

---

[13] Adjustments in the schedule may increase the number of freelancers in production departments. The interviews show that time delays in upper processes are routinely absorbed by shortening the production time allotted to lower processes. In the case of a TV animated series production, the production time allotted for the drawing processes, such as the key picture, animation picture, and coloring stages, is approximately 2 weeks; however, the process can be compressed into 1 week or even 3 days. To meet these shortened deadlines, studios must increase the number of workers in these lower processes.

Table 2.5 Important criteria for employing regular employees

Items	Responses
Positive attitude about the job	35
Communication skills	24
Cooperation in a team	20
Skills above a specific level	19
Rich creativity	18
Adaptation to the severe working environment	13
Working experience in the animation industry	5
Knowledge in multiple fields	4
Others	1
Unspecified	1

Source: Questionnaire survey
Forty-seven studios replied with multiple answers

Table 2.6 Opportunities for skill learning among freelancers

Opportunities	Responses
Acquiring skills at educational establishments	13
Guidance on the job from senior staff members	11
Acquiring skills through self-education after joining the industry	2
Training at previous studio	2
Training at current studio	2

Source: Questionnaire survey
Twenty freelancers replied with multiple answers

respondents), and one nonrespondent. This indicates that a large proportion of freelancers are graduates from technical schools, as is the case among regular employees.

When asked why they chose to freelance for their job style, freelancers responded both positively and negatively. Positive results were variations on "I can utilize my skills" (7 out of 20 respondents), "I can choose my work" (four respondents), and "there are few time constraints" (three respondents). Negative results were "no specific reason" (seven respondents), "worsening of interpersonal relationship" and "the intentions of the studio with which I am associated." In fact, most freelancers' motives contain a mixture of positive and negative reasons involving self-actualization through use of their skills and inevitable external factors.

Table 2.6 enumerates the various opportunities that freelancers have to acquire technical skills. The major opportunities are "acquiring skills at educational establishments" (13 respondents) and "guidance on the job from senior staff members" (11 respondents). This result indicates the importance of technical schools as a supply source of workers. In addition, the prevalence of "guidance on the job from senior staff members" shows that on-the-job skill learning is achieved not only through training provided by the studios, but also through vertical interpersonal

Table 2.7 Distribution of students at a special animation school by high school location

Local regions	Tokyo base	(%)	Osaka branch	(%)	Total	(%)
Hokkaido	3	(1.0)	2	(0.9)	5	(1.0)
Tohoku	23	(8.1)	1	(0.4)	25	(4.8)
Kanto	192	(65.1)	1	(0.4)	193	(37.2)
Chubu	44	(14.9)	6	(2.7)	50	(9.6)
Kinki	4	(1.4)	166	(74.1)	170	(32.8)
Chugoku	5	(1.7)	25	(11.2)	30	(5.8)
Shikoku	8	(2.7)	13	(5.8)	21	(4.0)
Kyushu	15	(5.1)	10	(4.5)	25	(4.8)
Total	295	(100.0)	224	(100.0)	519	(100.0)

Source: Interview survey

relationships between workers.[14] Furthermore, high rates of reemployment within the industry and the superiority of a technical school qualification show that this industry requires its workers to have high skill levels.

We can see the importance of technical schools as a main source of new labor. The site locations of 84 schools with courses for animators posted on RecruitSchool. net[15] (as of September 2, 2005) were analyzed to investigate the distribution of technical schools. Technical schools were located in 23 wards in Tokyo (20 schools), Osaka City (12 schools), Nagoya City (9 schools), and other major cities across the country. In the case of an animation school in Tokyo with a branch located in Osaka, students enrolled at the Tokyo base were from the Kanto region (65.1 %) and the Chubu region (14.9 %), while those at the Osaka branch were from the Kinki region (74.1 %) and the Chugoku region (11.2 %) (Table 2.7). The locations of the high schools attended by freshmen at the technical schools were restricted within narrow areas centered on the cities where the technical schools are located. The hometowns of freelancers, in contrast, were widely distributed across the country, including the Kanto region (nine respondents), the Shikoku region (three respondents), the Tohoku region (two respondents), the Hokuriku region (two respondents), the Tokai region (two respondents), Hokkaido (one respondent), and the Kyushu region (one respondent). Among respondents from the Kanto region, two freelancers each were from Tokyo, Kanagawa, Saitama, and Ibaraki prefectures, and one was from Tochigi Prefecture. This means that the proportion of freelancers who are originally from Tokyo is not high. In addition, an interview with one studio revealed that studios

---

[14] One interviewee referred to a senior worker (hereafter "X") who had taught him skills as his "master." Likewise, he referred to himself as an "X-*monka*" (descendent of X) and as from the "X-*juku*" (the school of X). Even though the interviewee is not currently taught by X, he still has a personal relationship with X.

[15] This is one of portal sites of education institutes targeted students preparing for entrance examinations. Students collect information about institutions they want to enter through this site. The site name was changed to Shingakunet. See http://shingakunet.com/ (accessed February 1, 2014).

scout for capable new talent among current students by sourcing out their animators as teachers at the technical schools.[16] For these reasons, technical schools act as the gateway to the animation industry, at least for provincials.

2.4.2 Social Relationships of Freelancers

2.4.2.1 Supply System of Freelancers

Approximately 65 % of payment to freelancers is based on their productivity; studios do not guarantee them a minimum wage (Table 2.8). This particularly unstable payment system is very common among workers in the "key picture" and "rendering" fields.

Table 2.8 Freelancer salary characteristics by field

Job fields	Length of service	Monthly income	Type of payment
Planning	10–	20–	Fixed
Director	5–10	15–20	Fixed
Director	5–10	20–	Fixed
Director	5–10	20–	Percentage
Director	10–	15–20	Piecework
Rendering	5–10	15–20	Piecework
Rendering	10–	20–	Fixed
Rendering	10–	20–	Piecework
Rendering	10–	20–	Piecework
Key picture	1–3	10–15	Piecework
Key picture	3–5	5–10	Piecework
Key picture	3–5	10–15	Piecework
Key picture	3–5	15–20	Piecework
Key picture	3–5	15–20	Piecework
Key picture	3–5	15–20	Piecework
Key picture	5–10	10–15	Piecework
Key picture	10–	20–	Piecework
Coloring	1–3	5–10	Percentage
Coloring	3–5	15–20	Piecework
Coloring	10–	15–20	Piecework

Source: Questionnaire survey
Workers in "planning" includes "planning and director" and "key picture" includes "key picture and coloring." "Monthly income" is in 1,000-yen units

---

[16]According to one technical school's literature and as confirmed in an interview, the school tries to enhance its value by inviting active creators from famous animation studios. For technical school students, this is not only an opportunity to meet successful animators in person, but also a chance to be scouted and join the industry earlier than others. This relationship between studios and technical schools is beneficial for both sides. Moreover, technical schools function as the entry point to the animation industry.

The distribution of salaries shows that 65 % of workers (13 respondents) receive less than 200,000 yen monthly. Seven out of the eight "key picture" workers receive less than 200,000 yen, while three out of the four "rendering" workers earn more than that. Despite the fact that a freelancer's working hours and workload are unstable, none of those surveyed had a second job.[17]

The relationship between duration of employment and salary explains why workers with less than 5 years of employment, who tend to work only in "key picture" and "coloring," have smaller salaries, while workers with 5–10 years' experience work in "key picture," "rendering," and "director." More than 10 years of employment enables workers to choose a career path, which helps them become specialists in "key picture," "coloring," "rendering," "director," or "planning." Furthermore, the interview results suggested that low wages in the "animation picture," "key picture," and "coloring" jobs lead to a high separation rate among young workers in the early stages of their careers.

2.4.2.2   Opportunities for Freelancers to Obtain Work

Although most freelancers received orders exclusively from one studio, some did receive orders from several studios. Table 2.9 shows that, on average, each freelancer received orders for 2.7 titles from 1.7 studios in October 2005. One freelancer responded that he received ten titles from five studios in a single month, and nine out of the 20 freelancers had more than one friend who could act as an intermediary for obtaining work. Based on the number of intermediaries, studios and titles, it can be concluded that the relationship between freelancers in the "key picture" or "rendering" fields and the studios is flexible. In addition, an interview with a former director indicated that freelancers are beneficial to the studios because their use requires directors to maintain connections with many freelancers; this helps studios to produce animated films with the expected product quality and maintain a necessary workforce along with their flexibility. Thus directors routinely try to build closer ties with freelancers by supplying them with jobs. Directors sometimes offer jobs to freelancers in slow seasons.[18] Moreover, freelancers in the creative and

---

[17] According to the result of statistical survey by National Tax Agency in 2006, the average annual income in 2005 of wage earners in their early 20s was 2.67 million yen, while that of those in their late 20s was 3.77 million yen. Average annual income categorized according to duration of employment shows that employees who have worked for 4 years or less earn 3.88 million yen annually. The two industries with the lowest average annual income are agriculture, forestry and fisheries, and the mining industry, tied at 3.04 million yen. Compared with these data, the income of freelancers reported in this chapter is not extraordinarily high.

[18] An interviewee stated that his studio's directors have a list called a "telephone directory," which contains the telephone numbers of other studios and workers. Directors telephone freelancers to ask them if they want work. Another interviewee working as a director emphasized the "thickness of the 'telephone directory' and the courage that it takes to call" freelancers to get help with the studio's work while not running out of orders. This director recognizes the importance of maintaining the studio's cultivated connections and the necessity of making new connections.

Table 2.9 Staff work situations in 1 month

Job fields	Connections (persons)	Studios	Titles
Planning	3	1	3
Director	0	1	1
Director	0	1	1
Director	0	3	3
Director	5	1	2
Rendering	0	1	1
Rendering	6	2	2
Rendering	Many	3	3
Rendering	Unknown	2	2
Key picture	0	1	3
Key picture	0	1	1
Key picture	3	1	4
Key picture	3	2	2
Key picture	3	3	4
Key picture	5	5	10
Key picture	5	2	3
Key picture	One studio	1	2
Coloring	0	1	2
Coloring	0	1	3
Coloring	0	1	2

Source: Questionnaire survey

production departments, such as "key picture" and "rendering," are sometimes offered jobs in similar situations. The reason why freelancers in the "key picture" and "rendering" departments can obtain jobs from several studios seems to be part of a risk-avoidance strategy against unstable employment. In addition, because "key picture" is earlier along the career path than "rendering," freelancers in "rendering" obtain work using connections made when they worked in "key picture" or before then (See also Chap. 5).

The tendency of workers to rely on connections with particular people was also seen as a reason for freelancers to continue to work in Tokyo. Sixteen out of the 20 freelancers answered negatively concerning any intentions to continue to work in the animation industry while moving out of the Tokyo area. The major reasons for continuing to work in Tokyo consist of the following (Table 2.10): the general economy of agglomeration, including such factors as "large number of production studios" (12 respondents) and "convenient transportation" (seven respondents); personal connection/personal preferences, such as "ease of obtaining inside industry information" (seven respondents), "presence of person I want to work with" (five respondents), and "large number of colleagues" (five respondents).[19] Given the fact that a large number of colleagues is thus regarded as a considerable benefit and given what we have seen regarding the skill-teaching relationships among workers, it can be concluded that developing personal networks is an important resource for freelancers whose employment status is unstable.

[19] The others include one worker from Tokyo and one not specified (one respondent).

	Reasons	Responses
Table 2.10 Freelancers' reasons for continuing to work in Tokyo	Large number of production studios	12
	Ease of obtaining inside industry information	7
	Convenient transportation	7
	Large number of colleagues	5
	Presence of person I want to work with	5
	Ease of enjoying services on the job	2
	Availability of many side jobs	1
	Attractiveness of Tokyo itself	1
	Others	2

Source: Questionnaire survey
Twenty freelancers replied with multiple answers

2.5 Conclusion

This chapter examined the agglomeration structure of the animation industry in Tokyo from the perspectives of business transactions and the labor market. The agglomeration of the animation industry in Japan consists of an interplay of the following four factors: (1) animation studios; (2) workers; (3) clients and related content industries; and (4) technical schools. An illustration of the model of this agglomeration in Tokyo is provided in Fig. 2.10.

Animation studios can be categorized into two types: primary contractor studios, which produce and manage animation projects; and professional subcontractor studios, which receive orders for specialized processes. Many clients, such as TV stations, publishers, and video game developers, are concentrated in Tokyo. In general, primary contractors establish fixed relationships with clients located in the CBD and relay most of their orders between firms outside and inside the industry. Thus animation studios agglomerate in Tokyo to achieve a close proximity to their clients.

In the industry, business transactions between partners depend on short delivery times, even as short as 1 day, and the contents of the transactions are fluid. These transaction characteristics make it difficult to record contract details. Therefore, studios generally do not make contract documents, yet they must mutually trust one another because of the risk of uncertainty associated with successfully completing a contract. Mutual trust and flexible transactions between business partners in the same industry sustain the agglomeration of animation studios in western Tokyo. In the case of primary contractors, although their main clients are located in the CBD, their business is more often conducted with others in the same industry than with their main clients, so primary contractors, too, tend to be located in western Tokyo.

In addition, some studios have formed international relationships with overseas animation production studios, such as South Korean or Chinese studios, to compensate for their lack of complementary skills and labor shortages. They have developed coordinated transportation systems, such as professional delivery and association delivery, making it possible for work to be delivered in person on the

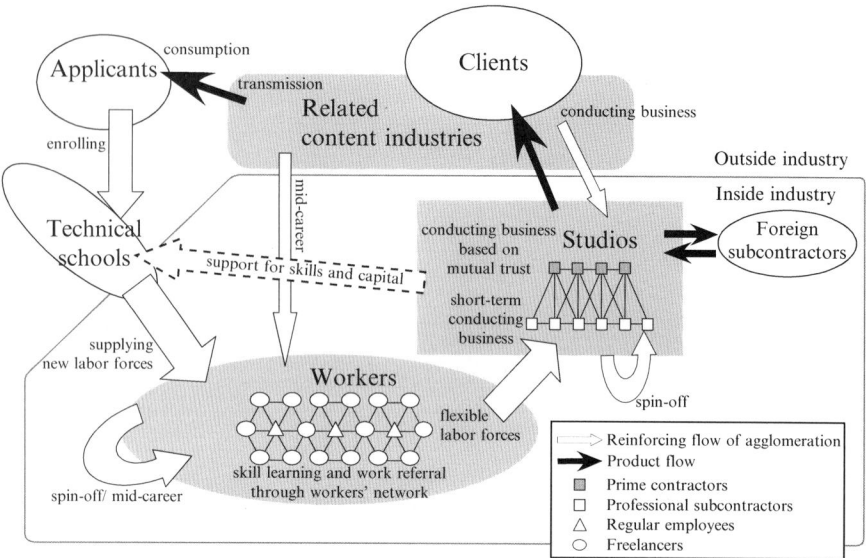

Fig. 2.10 Agglomeration structure of the animation industry in Tokyo

day of its completion. Access to other Japanese studios operating these delivery systems and access to an international airport are defining elements for the agglomeration of the animation industry in metropolises.

As for the labor market, most of the incoming workers and new graduates either leave the industry or are reemployed as experienced workers or freelancers. Freelancers, including both new graduates from technical schools and experienced workers from other studios, accept parts of the animation process as subcontract work to maintain their skills and have flexible employment. Freelancers acquire skills and receive on-the-job training from senior workers. They obtain jobs through personal connections both within and outside the studios to avoid income instability. Furthermore, freelancers are essential to the Japanese animation industry, partly because of the way in which the industry has specialized. The abovementioned skill learning systems and the avoidance of instability through networking are both easily available to freelancers in Tokyo, as many animators live in Tokyo and thus have access to each other, especially at work.

The market for animation has expanded all over Japan. Some animation fans in Japan hope to work in the animation business one day, perhaps entering the industry through one of the technical schools, which are the largest source of labor. Technical schools also play a role in gathering freshmen from rural areas and turning them into skilled workers. Furthermore, animation studios and technical schools have relationships in which the studios send workers to serve as teachers in order to find new talent. Only a few animators come to the industry from related content industries.

The agglomeration in western Tokyo is sustained and strengthened by mutual interactions between the constituent actors in the animation industry in Tokyo.

References

Arai Y, Nakamura H, Sato H, Nakazawa T, Sugizaki K (2004) Multimedia and Internet business clusters in central Tokyo. Urban Geogr 25:483–500. doi:10.2747/0272-3638.25.5.483

Association of Japanese Animations (2012) Anime Sangyo Repoto 2012 [Report of animation industry 2012]. Association of Japanese Animations, Tokyo (Japanese)

Hara S (2005) Gurobaru Kyoso Jidai ni okeru Nihon no Dejitaru Kontentsu Sangyo Shuseki no Kyoso Yuisei to Inobeshon no Hokosei - SD Gandamu Fosu Purojekuto o Jirei ni [Competitive advantage and innovation of digital content industrial clusters in Japan in global competition era: a case of "SD GUNDAMFORCE" project]. Ann Jpn Assoc Econ Geogr 51:368–386 (Japanese)

Konagaya K, Tomizawa K (eds) (1999) Maruchimedia Toshi no Senryaku: Shirikon Are to Maruchimedia Garuchi [The strategy adopted by multimedia cities: the cases of silicon alley and Multimedia Gulch]. Toyo keizai shinposha, Tokyo (Japanese)

Milgrom P, Roberts J (1992) Economics, organization & management. Prentice Hall, New Jersey

Sudo T (2008) Dai4sho Dejitaru Kontentsu no Bunyabetsu Doko 2 Animeshon [Chapter 4 The trend of major content industries, Section 2 Animation]. In: Digital Content Association of Japan (ed) Dejitaru Kontentsu Hakusho 2008 [Digital contents white paper 2008], pp 94–95 (Japanese)

The National Tax Agency (2006) Minkan Kyuyo Zittai Tokei Chosa [the statistical survey of actual status for salary in the private sector 2005]. The National Tax Agency, Tokyo (Japanese)

Washiya T (2004) Animeshon Seisaku [Animation production]. In: Ministry of Economy, Trade and Industry (ed) Kontentsu Porudusu Kino no Kyoka ni kansuru Chosa Kenkyu: Animeshon Seisaku [The research about the base reinforcement of the contents produce function: animation production]. Ministry of Economy, Trade and Industry, Tokyo, pp 17–18

Williamson OE (1983) Markets and hierarchies. Free Press, New York

Yamaguchi Y (ed) (2004) Dai3sho Sengo no Fukko kara Terebi Anime e [Chapter 3 From postwar reconstruction to TV animation]. In Nihon no Anime Zenshi: Sekai o Seishita Nihon Anime no Kiseki [Complete history of Japanese animation – the Miraculous and Global Domination by Japanese animation], Ten-Books, Tokyo, pp 63–88 (Japanese)

Yamamoto K (2012a) International production allocation strategies of Japanese animation studios. In: Schlunze RD, Agola NO, Baber WW (eds) Spaces of international economy and management: launching a new perspective on management and geography. Palgrave-MacMillan, Hampshire, pp 239–253

Yamamoto K (2012b) Animeshon Sangyo no Bungyo Kankei to Chiiki Seisaku [Division of labor relationships and local policies]. In: Tsunatoshi I, Masaya Y (eds) Sangyo Shuseki no Henbo to Chiiki Seisaku: Gurokaru Jidai no Chiiki Sangyo Kenkyu [The changes of industrial agglomeration and local polices – studies for local industries in the glocal era]. Minerva Shobo, Kyoto, pp 195–215 (Japanese)

Chapter 3
Agglomeration of the Animation Industry in Seoul, South Korea

Abstract This chapter examines the characteristics of the transactional relationships and the labor market that determine the agglomeration structure of the animation industry in Seoul, South Korea. Studios are classified into three groups according to their major business partners: those with Japanese clients, those with Western clients, and those with domestic clients. Studios of all types transact with other studios for complementary labor and techniques, and workers learn skills through their personal connections, as they do in the Japanese animation industry. Nevertheless, a more detailed examination reveals that different agglomeration structures have formed in Seoul because the industry in South Korea has developed as a subcontracting industry for Japan and the West, and each studio demands different specializations from its employees.

Keywords Foreign clients • International division of labor • Labor market • Seoul • South Korea

3.1 Introduction

This chapter examines the development and agglomeration of the animation industry in Seoul, South Korea. The South Korean animation industry has developed because of the international division of labor in relation to the Japanese and Western animation industries. Even today, the South Korean animation industry owes its existence to subcontracted production for the animation industry overseas. As a result, different agglomeration factors are at play compared with the Japanese animation industry, which has developed through domestic market demand. To understand the urban agglomeration of the South Korean animation industry, it is necessary to shed light on the international division of labor as presented in Chap. 1 in relation to the overseas expansion of the US film industry.

The examination was conducted using a questionnaire survey and interviews with animation studios in Seoul, as well as a questionnaire survey with the staff of these studios. Between June and July 2005, questionnaires were mailed to a sample

© Springer Japan 2014   45
K. Yamamoto, *The Agglomeration of the Animation Industry in East Asia*,
International Perspectives in Geography: AJG Library 4,
DOI 10.1007/978-4-431-55093-8_3

of 276 studios that were selected because of their location (described further in this chapter). Of these studios, nine (3.2 %) provided valid responses. The results of this survey do not completely illuminate the South Korean animation industry because of its low response rate. However, as stated in Sect. 3.2.2, the South Korean animation industry relies heavily on subcontracted work from overseas. According to Lent (1998), most South Korean animation production studios are small. Most studios that responded also showed similar capital size and transactions, as discussed later in this chapter (Sect. 3.3.1). Studios that responded can be considered to represent a portion of the structure of South Korean animation production studios and are suitable for investigation.

In addition to the questionnaire survey, interviews were conducted with another eight studios in March 2006 and 2008. From these interviews, valid data were obtained from six studios. Between June 2006 and January 2007 and in March and May 2008, a questionnaire survey was conducted with the staff of cooperating studios. Responses were obtained from 94 staff members. These survey results are used in the analysis below.

3.2 Development of the Animation Industry in Seoul

3.2.1 Evolution of the Number of TV Animation Shows in South Korea

Figure 3.1 shows the annual changes in the minutes of TV animation shows and that of animated movie releases as of the time of the study. Animated movies have been screened in the cinemas in South Korea since the second half of the 1960s and

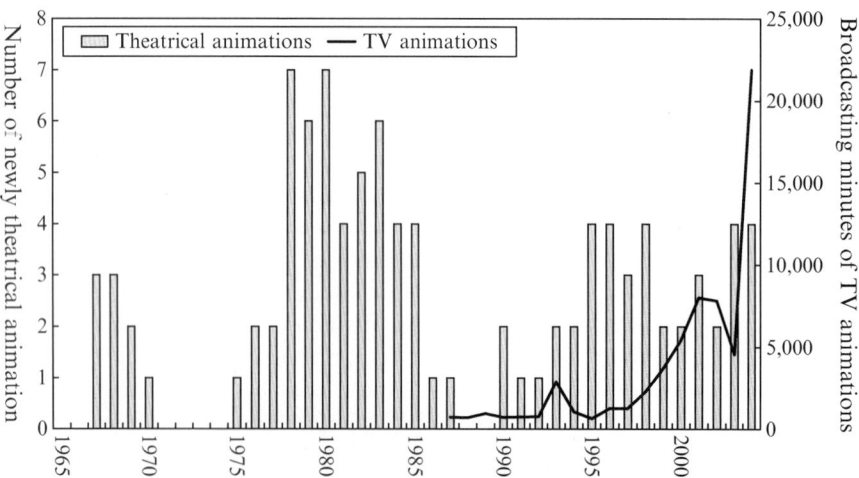

Fig. 3.1 Broadcast minutes devoted to animated TV programs and number of new animated programs in South Korea in 1965–2004. *Note*: Owing to the summary method of the source, any animation series that was broadcast for several years is counted in the year in which the series started. *Source*: Based on "KAPA 2004 Animation Information Book"

peaked in the 1980s (seven were screened in 1978 and 1980). Until the first half of the 1980s, animated movies were the main product of the industry in the domestic market, partly because of the low level of TV ownership.

According to the Korea Culture & Contents Agency (2004), animated movies made their first appearance in South Korea in 1957 with a Walt Disney movie. For the next 10 years, all animated movies were imported from the United States. Then, in 1967, the first domestically produced feature-length animated movie was released.

In contrast, TV animation started around 1970, with TV stations Korean Broadcasting System (KBS), Tongyang Broadcasting Company (TBC), and Munhwa Broadcasting Corporation (MBC) broadcasting foreign imported animations. Accordingly, airtime of animations on TV increased (Fig. 3.1). The broadcasting of domestic TV animation started in 1987. While TV animation had been limited to stand-alone products as specialized programs until then, KBS started running a weekly animation series in 1989.

According to the Korea Cultural & Contents Agency (2005), the annual number of minutes of animation aired by the three terrestrial TV stations (excluding Educational Broadcasting System [EBS]) in 2004 was 28,251. This number can be broken down into 15,968 min (56 %) for animations produced in South Korea and 12,283 min (44 %) for foreign productions. Airtime for South Korean-made animations exceeded that for foreign productions at KBS1 (81.4 %), KBS2 (51.8 %), and MBC (73.7 %). However, at Seoul Broadcasting System (SBS), airtime for foreign-made animations totaled 51 %. Furthermore, airtime for South Korean-made animations at EBS and three cable TV stations[1] was 21.9 % (EBS), 28.7 % (Tooniverse), 11.5 % (Anyone TV), and 1.1 % (Daekyo Kids TV). The reason why South Korean-made animations accounted for a majority of airtime at the three terrestrial TV stations (KBS, MBC and SBS) was that these stations observed the provisions on terrestrial broadcasting called "Bangsong Peurogeuraem Pyeonseong Biyurgosi (Notice on compilation ratio of broadcast programs)".[2] On the other hand, cable TV stations, for their part, were not able to comply with these provisions (Korea Culture & Contents Agency 2005).

One of the possible reasons why cable TV stations could not comply with these provisions is that the production of animations for the domestic market by domestic producers was small. According to Kim (2001), South Korean-made animations showed only modest economic success both within and outside South Korea because of the following five issues: (1) lack of highly creative staff; (2) a small-scale domestic

[1] EBS is a terrestrial TV station that broadcasts educational programs. Tooniverse and Anyone TV are cable TV stations that specialize in animations, and Daekyo Kids TV specializes in programs for children.

[2] The notice states the following: "In the case of domestically produced animations: (a) terrestrial broadcasting operators: more than 45 % of all animation airtime; (b) broadcasting stations other than terrestrial operators: more than 40 % of all animation airtime; (c) regardless of provisions (a) and (b), more than 8 % for operators specializing in programs relating to education and more than 4 % for operators specializing in programs relating to religion." See http://old.kcc.go.kr/user.do?m ode=view&page=P05030200&dc=K04030000&boardId=1063&boardSeq=14118 (last access on April 9, 2014) for more detailed information.

market where investment-return is troublesome; (3) difficulty in developing business for domestically produced animations in foreign markets because of a lack of high-quality stories; (4) lack of investment related to domestic production; and (5) an inadequate system of proactive and efficient cooperation in the areas of production and business. Items (2), (4), and (5) are issues relating to investment risk because of market size, while items (1) and (3) are those concerning production methods.

Therefore, we show the state of development of the South Korean animation industry as set forth below, focusing on the size of the market and the production system of products.

3.2.2 Scale of the South Korean Animation Industry

According to the Japan External Trade Organization (2007), revenues from animation and the related character industry, together with licensing revenues, in South Korea are estimated from 350 million dollars in 2003 to 550 million dollars in 2005. Sales of animation productions and copyright earnings amounted to 92.4 % (2004) of the total. In comparison, market size of the Japanese animation industry totaled 224.4 billion yen (approximately 2.054 billion dollars) in 2005 (The Association of Japanese Animations 2012).[3] While a simple comparison cannot be made because of differences in calculation methods, it is apparent that as of 2005, the market size of the South Korean animation industry was less than a quarter of that of the Japanese animation industry.

Regarding the characteristics of the South Korean animation industry, the Korea Culture & Contents Agency (2004) notes that (1) Japanese-made animation accounts for the largest share of products circulating in the South Korean-domestic market and (2) subcontracted production from overseas accounts for the largest share of revenues of animation studios. Table 3.1 provides a breakdown of the annual revenues, imports, and exports of the South Korean animation industry by business segment. Table 3.1 shows that 52.2 % (106.66 million dollars) of the total revenue depend on foreign transactions. In particular, "subcontracted production" from overseas (41.5 %) represents the largest share. In contrast, "creative production/copyright" (26.0 %) represents a large share of domestic sales, which account for 48 % of the total revenue. "Subcontracted production" accounts for 89 % (74.5 million dollars) of the total exports amount. Of the 50 animations representing subcontracted products from overseas markets, Japan accounts for 17 (34.0 %); United States, 12 (24.0 %); France, nine (18.0 %); Canada, five (10.0 %); and other countries, seven (14.0 %). With regard to the import amount, "creative production/copyright" tops the list at 98.3 % (5.23 million dollars), showing that finished products are the special focus of import transactions.

---

[3] Calculated as 100 yen = 0.96 US dollars as of January 3, 2005.

Table 3.1 Sales, exports/imports, and the number of subcontracted works in the South Korean animation industry

Job type	Sales						Value of trade	
	Total		Domestic		Overseas		Export	Import
Copyright/ creative	70,119	(34.3)	53,083	(26.0)	17,008	(8.3)	8,173	5,228
Subcontract	99,353	(48.6)	14,495	(7.1)	84,850	(41.5)	74,504	0
Sub-sub contract	1,300	(0.6)	968	(0.5)	332	(0.2)	348	0
Post production	789	(0.4)	798	(0.4)	0	(0.0)	0	0
Distribution services	32,483	(15.9)	27,999	(13.7)	4,469	(2.2)	276	0
Marketing/ Publication	–	–	–	–	–	–	0	91
Others	1,050	(0.1)	303	(0.1)	0	(0.0)	0	0
Total	204,305	(100.0)	97,647	(47.8)	106,658	(52.2)	83,301	5,319

Source: Based on Korea Creative & Content Agency (2010)
One dollar=936 won
Numbers in parentheses indicate component percentages
Job types are based on the source referenced below
This table is based on a questionnaire survey administered at 163 South Korean animation studios by the Korea Creative Content Agency in 2009
Unit: 1,000 dollars

Table 3.2 Recent changes in sales in the South Korean animation industry by business type and media from 2007 to 2009

Business from		TVs	Movies	Packages	The Internet	New media	Others	Total
Domestic	Copyright	3.6	–	–	29.3	–	–	7.6
	Creative	18.9	–14.5	–29.3	–6.0	209.3	11.9	13.8
	Subcontracted	18.4	–15.3	9.9	20.8	229.0	–36.9	5.5
Overseas	Copyright	5.3	–	41.7	–	–	–	5.3
	Creative	159.2	–	27.9	–	–	72.9	120.4
	Subcontracted	–20.9	81.4	–9.2	–	–	–	–15.9

Source: Based on "2010 Animation industry white paper" by the Korea Culture & Contents Agency (2010), Table 3-1-27, Table 3-1-28, Table 3-1-29
Note: "–" indicates data not available
Unit: %

The South Korean animation industry relies heavily on subcontracted production from Japan and the West, as described above. Incidentally, recent years have seen both an enlargement of the South Korean domestic market and the expansion of South Korean production companies into foreign markets. Table 3.2 shows the percentage change in revenues by media category of the South Korean animation industry between 2007 and 2009. Table 3.2 shows that creative (18.9 %) and subcontracted (18.4 %) production for new media (mobile phones, Internet protocol TV, digital multimedia broadcasting) in particular saw remarkable revenue growth

Table 3.3 South Korean animation industry sales in 2009 by media

	TVs	Movies	Packages	The Internet	New media	Others	Total
Domestic	130,086	10,647	13,879	8,101	20,014	4,876	187,603
Overseas	84,121	1,720	11,042	163	–	6,740	103,786
Total	214,207	12,367	24,921	8,264	20,014	11,616	291,389
Ratio	73.5 %	4.2 %	8.6 %	2.8 %	6.9 %	4.0 %	100.0 %

Source: Based on the Korea Culture & Contents Agency (2010), Table 3-1-26
Note: "–" indicates data not available
Unit: billion Won

in relation to domestic operations and creative production (159.2 %) compared with overseas operations. Furthermore, a reduction in overseas subcontracting (−20.9 %) can be observed. The new media market opened up through the spread of digital devices, and its size has expanded rapidly from 1.9 billion won in 2007, to 9.4 billion won in 2008, to 20 billion won in 2009. However, the TV ratio, at 73.5 % (214.2 billion won), remains a significant source of revenue for the industry (Table 3.3).

One possible reason why production companies in the South Korean animation industry have been able to increase their share of products for the domestic market and expand into foreign markets at the same time is that technology development through subcontracted production for foreign companies has reached a certain level. Another reason may be that policies to support the domestic content industry, such as broadcasting regulations by the South Korean government for foreign products, have shown effectiveness in recent years.

3.2.3 Distribution of Animation Studios in South Korea

According to a Paran telephone directory search, one of South Korean famous online telephone directory at the time of survey,[4] there were 164 studios in the categories "animation production businesses" and "cartoon movie production businesses," of which 122 (74.4 %) are located in Seoul. Furthermore, a search for animation production studios using the "2004 Korea Animation Corporation Directory," "Korean Animation Producers Association (KAPA) 2004 Animation Information Book," and KAPA member company presentations[5]—in addition to the Paran telephone directory search—identified 276 studios in Seoul. Figure 3.2 shows the distribution of the identified studios. While the studios are distributed such that they surround Jung Ward with its numerous governmental administrative agencies,

---

[4] http://local.paran.com/, last accessed on July 6, 2008. The site had been closed now.
[5] KAPA member company presentations are on KAPA's Web site (http://www.koreaanimation.or.kr/, last accessed on July 6, 2008).

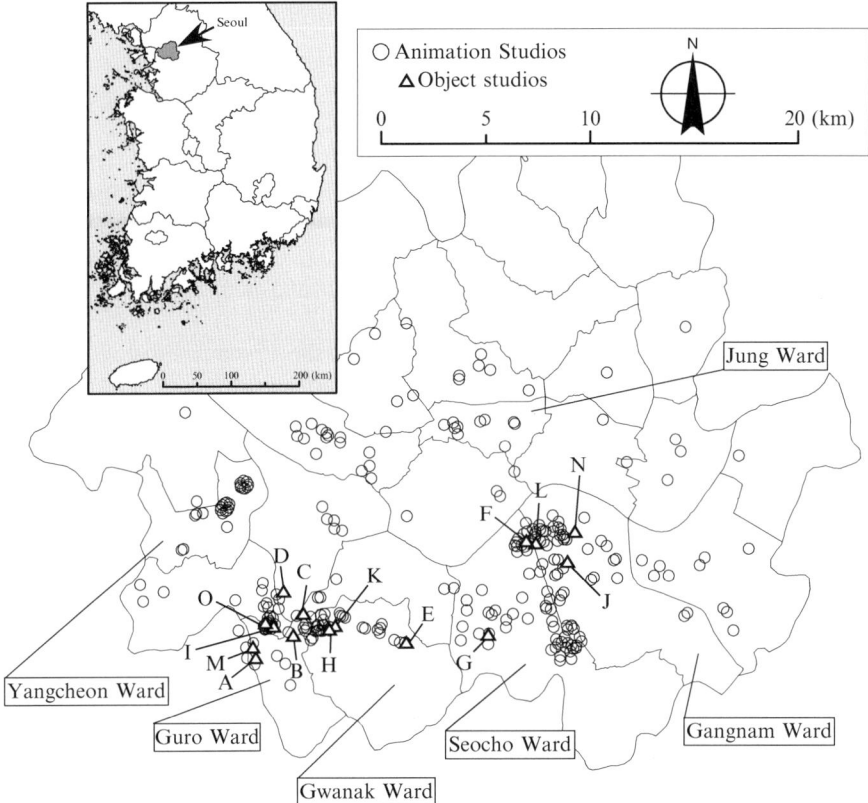

Fig. 3.2 Locations of animation studios and participating studios in Seoul. *Source*: Paran telephone number search, "2004 Korea animation corporation directory," and "KAPA 2004 Animation Information Book," KAPA member company presentation

there also appear to be concentrations in Sillim-dong, Gwanak Ward (28 studios) in the southwest. Concentrations in the southeast are found in Jamwon-dong, Seocho Ward (seven studios); Sinsa-dong, Gangnam Ward (nine studios); and Yangjae-dong, Seocho Ward (15 studios). Other areas of concentration can be observed in Yangcheon Ward with Guro Digital Industrial Complex (ten studios), Hyundai Dream Town (nine studios), and Booyoung Greentown (eight studios).[6]

---

[6] Hyundai Dream Town and Booyoung Greentown are housing complexes where studios occupy apartments alongside other private citizens. There is a TV station in the vicinity, which suggests a related content industry agglomeration. The Guro Digital Industrial Complex, Hyundai Dream Town, and Booyoung Greentown are all properties that were subject to full-scale sale after 2000. Several studios moved in within several years, which suggests that production studios are highly mobile.

3.3   Characteristics of Interbusiness Transactions

3.3.1   Basic Studio Attributes

Tables 3.4 and 3.5 outline the basic attributes of the 15 studios surveyed. The results show that there are eight studios with a capital stock of less than one billion won.[7] This represents 67 % of the total, excluding three studios whose capital stock is unknown. Furthermore, ten studios (71 %) have 19 or fewer regular employees, suggesting that the majority of studios surveyed are small and medium-sized businesses (Table 3.4).

A review of major clients revealed that for 7 of the 15 studios that responded, orders from foreign studios accounted for over half their revenues. Furthermore, three of the six studios interviewed perceived foreign markets as their primary market (Table 3.5). These findings show that the surveyed studios share the general features of South Korean animation production studios pointed out in previous studies. Ten studios were found to be over 50 % dependent on foreign orders for their revenue, and three studios depended on domestic orders for more than half of their revenue.[8]

Table 3.4   Basic characteristics of participating studios

Studio	Establishment	Capital	Employees	Annual sales
A	1987	1,400	13	4,600
B	1989	180	20	1,800
C	1989	118	45	680
D	1990	–	2	–
E	1991	–	6	–
F	1994	2,200	16	350
G	1995	500	15	1,500
H	1998	50	5	110
I	1998	100	5	20
J	1999	875	50	900
K	2000	–	–	–
L	2001	150	10	700
M	2002	2,400	60	100
N	2002	187	14	300
O	2007	1,400	13	1,600

Source: Questionnaire survey and interview survey
Capital and annual sales are in one-million-won units
"Employees" refers only to regular employees
"–" indicates nondisclosure

[7] 100 won = 12.02 yen or 0.11 US dollars as of November 19, 2007.

[8] The responses on countries of overseas transactions and transaction details showed that one of these studios (Studio C) resembles studios that depend on orders from Japan for more than half of their work flow. Consequently, Studio C is treated here together with studios dependent on foreign orders.

Table 3.5 Business fields of foreign clients of participating studios

Studio	Category	Dependency rate for foreign clients (%)	Primary client		Secondary client		Subcontracted process										
			Country	Business field	Country	Business field	Planning	Directing	Rendering	Key picture	Animation picture	Coloring	Background	Shooting	Sound effect	Editing	Computer graphic
A	w	100	USA	An,F,B,M	USA	An,G,B,M				o	o	o	o	o			
B	j	100	JPN	An	–					o	o	o					
C	j	x	JPN	An	/			o	o	o	o	o	o	o	o		o
D	j	Major	JPN	An	/			o	o	o	o	o	o	o	o		o
E	j	Major	JPN	An	/							o		o			
F	d	1–25	FRA	An	–			o	o	o	o	o	o	o			
G		x	x		/		x										
H	j	51–75	JPN	An	JPN	An	o			o	o	o					
I	d	0	–		–		–										
J	w	76–99	ESP	M	USA	M	o				o	o	o	o			
K	j	Major	JPN	An	/		o		o		o	o	o	o		o	
L	d	1–25	USA	Ad	x		o		o	o	o	o	o	o	o	o	o
M	w	76–99	USA	An	–		o					o					o
N	w	76–99	USA	M	USA	M					o	o				o	o
O	j	76–99	JPN	An	JPN	An	o	o	o	o	o	o	o	o		o	o

Source: Questionnaire survey and interview survey

In the category column, "j" indicates that the studio has Japanese clients, "w" indicates Western clients, and "d" indicates domestic clients

The questionnaire asked each studio about its two biggest clients, while the interview survey asked only about the single most important client

Dependency rates for foreign clients are calculated based on the sales amount from foreign clients divided by the annual sales. "Major" indicates that the studio's major clients are foreign clients

In the country column: JPN, Japan; USA, United States of America; FRA, France; ESP, Spain

In the business fields column: An, animation production; F, film production; B, broadcasting; G, game creation; Ad, advertising; M, multimedia-related services; o, others

"/" indicates that the information was not requested in the survey

"–" indicates not applicable

"x" indicates no response or unknown

Client differentiation exists among the 11 studios dependent on foreign orders. Studios that receive orders from Japan do not receive orders from the West. Conversely, studios that receive orders from the West do not receive orders from Japan. Moreover, the industries in which their clients operate are different. Japanese companies specialize in animation production, whereas Western companies run not only animation production, but also related content industries, including multimedia-related services. The 11 studios dependent on foreign orders can be grouped as follows on the basis of the country where most orders originated: seven studios (B, C, D, E, H, K, O) in Japan, three (A, M, N) in the United States, and one (J) in Europe. Of the three studios that had mainly domestic clients, only one (I) operated exclusively in the domestic market. The other two studios (F, L) also received orders from Western companies.

The studios can be divided into broad categories. Studios mainly dependent on foreign orders are subdivided by countries of major clients into "studios with Japanese clients" (B, C, D, E, H, K, O) and "studios with Western clients" (A, J, M, N), whereas studios with mainly domestic orders are grouped into "studios with domestic clients" (F, I, L).

In relation to studio size by category, data on capital stock size were obtained from four of the seven studios in the case of orders from Japanese studios. The capital stock of two of these studios was under 200 million won. For studios with Western clients, the capital stock of three of the four studios exceeded 200 million won. For studios with domestic clients, the capital stock of two of the three studios was under 200 million won. As such, studios with Western clients have a large company size compared with those in other categories. In terms of regular employee numbers, four of the seven studios with Japanese clients mentioned that they have at least ten employees. The same response was received from all studios with Western clients and two of the three studios with domestic clients. The revenue of studios with Japanese clients except Studio A exceeds that of studios with Western clients and studios with domestic clients.[9]

As shown in Fig. 3.2 and Tables 3.4 and 3.5, many studios with Japanese clients were established in or before the first half of the 1990s (B, C, D, E). These studios are concentrated in Sillim-dong, Gwanak Ward in southwest Seoul (four out of six studios).[10] According to Studio B, production studios were concentrated in Sillim-dong, Gwanak Ward since pre-1990 for three main reasons. (1) A technical school (now defunct) that provided a source of labor was located near Sillim-dong, which made it easy to secure new employees. (2) It is essential to secure a labor force as

---

[9] Studio A mainly subcontracts work from several major US animation production studios. As of 2005, its entire revenue was earned through foreign orders. It has subcontracted work from US animation production studios since its inception. In the second half of the 1990s, it received prizes such as the Korean Prime Minister's Award for its sizeable exports.

[10] As for the two studios located outside Sillim-dong (C, D), Studio C moved to a neighboring district by considering the importance of proximity to other studios in the same business located around Sillim-dong. Initially located in Sillim-dong, Studio D moved away because of increased domestic work. It is now considering moving back because it is conscious of the importance of proximity to other studios in the same business.

Fig. 3.3 Background drawing at a studio with Japanese clients (2006). *Note*: Background draw-ings were first drawn by hand and then digitalized. Paints were made in Japan, and studios accom-modated each other when stocks run low

required in the production process, and being in the same location enabled production studios to share human resources. (3) Being in the same location also enabled pro-duction studios to lend materials to one another when their own material stocks were depleted, particularly when working for Japanese production studios who require that materials such as celluloid and paint all be Japanese products (Fig. 3.3).

Studios with Western clients and those with domestic clients were established mainly in the second half of the 1990s or later (I, J, L, M, N). The studios are located in CBDs such as Nonhyeon-dong, Gangnam Ward (J, L, N) and Jamwon-dong, Seocho Ward (F).[11] In this way, differences can be observed between the categories regarding trends in year of establishment and business location.

---

[11] The two studios located in districts other than Nonhyeon-dong, Gangnam Ward, and Jamwon-dong, Seocho Ward, (A, M) accept orders exclusively from a limited number of foreign companies (A: two companies; M: one company). These two studios are thought to have chosen their location by considering access to the international airport, and thereby temporal proximity to the foreign companies with which they operate exclusively. Meanwhile, satisfactory Internet facilities, spa-cious premises, and municipal government incentives were cited in interviews as reasons for mov-ing to the Guro Digital Industrial Complex.

3.3.2 Characteristics of Major Clients

In relation to the industry categories of major domestic and foreign clients, for all studios with Japanese clients except for Studio O, major domestic clients operate in animation production (Table 3.6).[12] Major foreign clients are also animation production studios (Table 3.5). By contrast, the major domestic clients of studios with Western clients do not conduct business with companies in animation production. Regarding major foreign clients, for studios with Western clients, those conducting business with companies categorized in animation production are Studios A and M (Table 3.5). In other words, for studios with Western clients, only half of the major domestic and foreign clients operate in animation production. However, there is a high incidence of business with companies in the related content industry such as the multimedia-related service and advertising industries. The major clients of

Table 3.6 Business fields of domestic clients of participating studios

	Primary client	Secondary client
Studio	Business fields	Business fields
A	–	–
B	–	–
C	Animation production, Broadcasting	–
D	Animation production	–
E	–	–
F	Animation production	Animation production
G	Animation production, Broadcasting, Multimedia-related services, Others	–
H	Animation production, Film production, Broadcasting	Animation production, Video game development, Advertising
I	Broadcasting	Film production
J	Multimedia-related services	Video game development
K	–	–
L	Animation production, Advertising, Multimedia-related services	Animation production, Film production, Advertising
M	–	–
N	Film production, Broadcasting, Advertising	Film production
O	Others	Others

Source: Questionnaire survey and interview survey
The questionnaire asked each studio about its two biggest clients, while the interview survey asked only about the single most important client
"–" indicates no response or unknown

---

[12] Studio O's domestic orders, which account for approximately 3 % of its total orders, are for the production of commercials for corporations in general.

Table 3.7 Reasons for site selection

Items	Japanese	Western	Domestic
Geographic proximity to studios in the same business	6	3	2
Good transportation access	5	2	2
Cheap rent	4	3	1
Geographic proximity to companies in related industries	–	–	2
Positive image of the locality	–	–	1
Easy acquisition of market information	–	3	1
Other	3		
Reply studios	7	4	3

Source: Questionnaire survey and interview survey
Note: Multiple answers were permitted. "Japanese" indicates that the studio serves Japanese clients, "Western" indicates Western clients, and "Domestic" indicates domestic clients

studios with domestic clients conduct business with companies in various industries including not only the animation industry, but also broadcasting, advertising, and film production industries.

Upon inquiry of the reasons for the choice of studio location, six of the seven studios with Japanese clients indicated having "geographic proximity to studios in the same business." Furthermore, five studios responded "good transportation access," four studios responded "cheap rent," and three studios responded "other" (Table 3.7). Studios with Japanese clients use association delivery and professional delivery when conducting business with Japanese production studios.[13] Moreover, Japanese production studios require short delivery times. Because of this particular feature of conducting business with Japanese production studios, studios with Japanese clients need easy access to the international airport (Incheon International Airport). (See also Chap. 2). At the same time, studios with Japanese clients continue to share labor with peer production studios,[14] so that all of them can remain flexible against the large fluctuations in production volumes required by Japanese studios.

However, as for studios with Western clients, "geographic proximity to studios in the same business," "cheap rent," and "good transportation access" are considered important in line with studios with Japanese clients. Three studios also mentioned "easy acquisition of market information," which was not cited by studios with Japanese clients. Studios with Western clients conduct business with the domestic companies in the related content industry, even although transaction dependency is low. It is suggested that seeking an environment in which it is easy to access infor-

---

[13] Data transfer with Japanese production studios also takes place using fax and Internet (file transfer protocol lines). The finished product can also be delivered directly to a studio by placing an order online. Even in such cases, the key and animation pictures produced by South Korean production studios are delivered by the person in charge of Japanese studios because of copyright issues for the key and animation pictures produced.

[14] Studio O places orders with a younger studio that used to be operated by Studio O and now operates independently. Also, Studio K places orders with a production studio run by brothers of Studio K's manager. Locally, such partners are referred to as "peers."

mation on the related content industry (i.e., proximity to information) along with geographic proximity to the related content industry. Furthermore, studios with Western clients are thought to focus on access to the international airport for international business.

Studios with domestic clients also consider proximity to studios in the same business and transportation access as important ("geographic proximity to studios in the same business," by two studios, and "good transportation access," by two studios). In this aspect, Studio L is an example; its main strength is planning and design work. When its workload is such that it cannot maintain the quality of the products through its own production, this studio places orders with a peer studio that is skilled in the production of animation pictures and computer graphics. Physical proximity to other studios in the same business (geographic proximity) and temporal proximity (good transportation access) appear in Studio L's response as reasons for its choice of location because of its regular contacts with other studios in the same business.

In the case of studios with domestic clients, one studio also cited "positive image of the locality." Regarding this point, we introduce the case of Studio F. In 1997, this studio moved its management function to Yangjae-dong, Seocho Ward, but integrated its directing department in Sillim-dong, Gwanak Ward in 1998. It then moved to its current location in Jamwon-dong, Seocho Ward, primarily because Jamwon-dong is adjacent to Gangnam Ward and the surrounding area has a good reputation. According to the studio, owning an office in such a district fosters the trust of the other companies, particularly Western companies, with which it conducts business.

Regarding proximity to the related content industry, there is a difference between studios with Western clients and those with domestic clients. The former studios focus on access to information. In contrast, the latter studios focus on both access to information and physical proximity to clients ("geographic proximity to companies in related industries," cited by two studios and "easy acquisition of market information," cited by one studio). This finding reflects the fact that studios with domestic clients frequently conduct face-to-face business with companies in the related content industry, which requires physical proximity.

In this way, both studios with Western clients and those with domestic clients have frequent business contacts with the related content industry. Therefore, the ability to foster trust through location, agglomeration of the related content industry, easy acquisition of information concerning this type of industry, and ample opportunities to conduct face-to-face business are why studios with Western clients and those with domestic clients chose locations in the city center.

3.3.3   Characteristics of Business Conditions

To gain a more detailed understanding of actual business conditions, studios were asked about the issues on which they focus when they accept orders from major clients. Many studios with Japanese clients mentioned the following issues: "Whether the work is in a field that the studio is good at" (three of the seven studios), "whether the studio can handle the assigned workload," "viable delivery time," and "trust regarding payment." "Building and maintaining personal relationships through business" and "conventional business relationship" were also cited. Studios with Japanese clients appear to consider their social relationship with Japanese production studios as important, in addition to maintaining product quality and volume. According to Studio K, it is not possible to conduct stable operations in the domestic market because of its small size. Consequently, the studio tends to depend on work from Japanese studios. In addition, business relationships established with Japanese production studios tend to be fixed. Moreover, because of the peer-based structure within which studios with Japanese clients construct, there is a tacit agreement to not steal Japanese production studios that are clients of other studios.

Also, in relation to "building and maintaining personal relationships through business," Studio K suggested that studios may conduct business even if they know that it is unprofitable, in order to build new personal relationships through contacts at Japanese production studios or to maintain existing relationships. Furthermore, Studio O suggested that studios may conduct small business trials when embarking on a new business. In doing so, they may add terms beneficial to the Japanese production studio such as providing products free of charge, if they do not meet the quality requirements of the Japanese production studio.

"Conventional business relationship" refers to the mutual understanding between the client and supplier for the smooth conduct of business, such as product quality and business methods, which are important to Japanese clients. Among the studios surveyed, there were some studios that dispatched mutual workers with Japanese production studios for mutual understanding at work sites to achieve smooth business. Thus, they have built fixed business relationship with specific studios for stable management and smooth business.

In contrast, all studios with Western clients responded that they focus on "whether the work is in a field that the studio is good at." Three of the four studios responded about "whether the studio can handle the assigned workload."[15] Among studios with domestic clients, two studios responded with "whether the work is in a field that the studio is good at," two studios responded "viable delivery time," and one studio responded "whether the studio can handle the assigned workload," in relation to business with major foreign clients. Neither the studios with Western clients nor those with domestic clients responded with "building and maintaining personal relationships through business," as was the case with studios with Japanese clients. According to Studio F, when conducting business with Western companies, they assess the counterpart based on indicators such as social trust, reputation within the industry, and business performance. Furthermore, these Western clients are particular about stable production volumes and product quality in order to gain their trust.

However, in relation to the domestic business of studios with domestic clients, two studios responded with "whether the work is in a field that the studio is good at"

---

[15] As for other responses, two studios responded "trust regarding payment," one studio responded "conventional business," and one studio responded "viable delivery time."

two studios responded "whether the studio can handle the assigned workload," and one studio responded "trust regarding payment." Further responses included "geographic proximity to the client" (one studio), "conventional business relationship," "high pay rate," and "favorable business conditions." These findings suggest that in relation to domestic business, fixed business relationships have been established because of the proximity to major clients.

Additionally, studios were asked whether they explicitly recorded contract details when conducting business. The results revealed that three of the four studios with Japanese clients would not do so, while all four studios with Western clients would do so. All three studios with domestic clients also responded that they would explicitly record contract details.

This difference in the way of business results from differences in clients' business activity. For studios with Japanese clients, business between studios in the same industry is the norm. In addition, in the Japanese TV market, animation generally begins to be aired before the completion of the final episode of a series. In Japanese TV animation, there can be changes to the schedule in the middle of the broadcast of a series depending on market response. Consequently, scheduling is difficult to define at the production site, and flexibility is considered essential in responding to circumstances.[16] Therefore, the explicit recording of contract details is troublesome for studios with Japanese clients when conducting business.

At the same time, the studios in the related content industry, in addition to the same type of industry, are major clients for both studios with Western clients and those with Japanese clients. As a result, the tacit agreement seen in business with other studios in the same business does not often hold, which makes the explicit recording of contract details essential. Additionally, according to the interviews, explicit recording not only vouches for the studio's trustworthiness, but also leads to a relationship of mutual trust with the client.

Many of the orders received are production department's processes, such as key picture, animation picture, and coloring, for studios in all categories (Table 3.5). Some studios also receive creative department orders, such as planning and rendering, and directing department. As opposed to studios with Western clients, some studios with Japanese clients enter into a gross contract for the production of an entire animation episode, from directing and rendering to editing with quality checking (Figs. 3.4 and 3.5).

Also, in relation to delivery time for the half-finished product to the issuer, all studios with Japanese clients, except for Studio C answered "1 day." There are instances where a studio on its own cannot manage the workload from Japanese studios. As noted earlier, in such cases, the studio manages by delegating part of the

---

[16] According to the interviews, it is usual in the animation industry for schedules to change suddenly and production delays in the upper process (the Japanese side) to be absorbed in the lower process (the South Korean side). Within such a production system, it is unclear who has responsibility. On the other hand, while the explicit recording of contract details clarifies where responsibility lies, it makes it difficult to respond to changes in circumstances. Consequently, the explicit recording of contract details can often result in disadvantages for both production studios.

Fig. 3.4 Animation picture quality check at a studio with Japanese clients (2006)

Fig. 3.5 Animation pictures waiting for quality check (2006). *Note*: This studio produces and inspects animation pictures based on key pictures transported from Japanese studios

work to another studio in the same business located in the vicinity.[17] Furthermore, according to Studio O, there are two types of orders from Japan. One is "scheduled work," which corresponds to a gross contract. The other is "nonscheduled work," which is part of the studio's production process. In the former case, there are checkpoints on the Japanese side in accordance with the stage of production, such as storyboard, key picture, and animation picture. Completed portions are sent to Japan and checked by the client. The checked product is sent back to South Korea. For nonscheduled work, the order received follows the schedule for association delivery or professional delivery within 3 days.

In contrast, in the case of studios with Western clients, the shortest delivery time is "1 month," and may exceed 2 months. According to Studio O, when planning an animation episode for a Western company, the product is delivered following the editing stage. There are only a few checks by the company placing the order in the intervening period. In the case of an animation series, the check is limited to the first few episodes. Western companies stop checking once they approve a given level of quality regarding the product. Such differences in the business systems appear as differences in delivery time.

The shortest delivery time for studios with domestic clients is also "1 month." Of these studios, the major clients in Studio I's domestic business are those in the broadcasting industry (Table 3.6). The foreign orders of Studios F and L include directing department and creative department work in addition to production department work. Based on these types of orders, the 1-month delivery time for studios with domestic clients is common where the gross contracting of animation products takes place.

3.4   Characteristics of the Labor Market

This section examines whether staff characteristics affect the agglomeration of production studios. The questionnaire survey focused on the staff of studios with Japanese clients and those with Western clients. Sixty-two of the 94 respondents were staff at three studios with Japanese clients and 32 were staff at four studios with Western clients.

---

[17] According to the interviews, somewhat unreasonable work must also be accepted to maintain the work flow from Japanese production studios. By responding to the demands of a Japanese production studio, a relationship of mutual trust is built and the studio's reputation with Japanese studios increases.

3.4.1 Staff Attributes

3.4.1.1 Basic Attributes

Concerning the type of staff employed in an animation studio, of the 62 respondents at the studios with Japanese clients, six are regular employees, 53 are freelancers, and three have other or unknown status. In contrast, in the case of the studios with Western clients, of the 32 respondents, nine are regular employees, 19 are freelancers, and four have other or unknown status. There are a large number of freelancers in both categories.

The breakdown of job fields for studios with Japanese clients is as follows: one producer, one director, two background, 47 key picture, eight coloring, and three other or unknown. Only one staff member performed multiple types of work. Some staff at studios with Japanese clients are specialists in specific production departments. However, in the case of studios with Western clients, nine of the 32 staff perform tasks such as producer, rendering, key picture, and animation picture. Four of the nine staff are regular employees, four are freelancers, and one has other status, which indicates that staff perform additional tasks regardless of their type of employment.

These differences in the type of work by staff are because of differences in the work undertaken by the production studios. In other words, business with Japanese studios requires production within a short timeframe, with staff focusing on their specific roles in the production department, such as key picture, animation picture, and coloring. For this reason, studios with Japanese clients try to raise production capacity by employing freelancers who specialize in specific processes. In contrast, studios with Western clients appoint the main staff members in charge of multiple types of work to maintain the quality and design required by clients.

Concerning the payment system, 51 of the 62 staff at studios with Japanese clients were paid based on their completed output. This figure indicates that this payment system is the norm. Of these staff, 50 were freelancers. In contrast, 13 of the 32 staff at studios with Western clients were paid based on their completed output, while 12 staff received a fixed salary. All regular employees received a fixed salary. In both categories, many staff members earned a monthly income of 1–1.5 million won. Thirty-four of the 62 staff at studios with Japanese clients and 12 of the 32 staff at studios with Western clients belonged to this group. As for the relationship between earnings and the number of years worked, staff monthly earnings increased according to the number of years worked in both categories (Table 3.8). However, when staff with the same number of years work, the monthly earnings of staff at studios with Western clients are higher than those of staff at studios with Japanese clients.

Table 3.8 Distribution of employees' monthly income and years of employment

Years of employment	Monthly income (Unit: 10,000 won)						
	<50	<100	<150	<200	200≤	Unknown	Total
<2	3/1	4/–	–/3	–/1			7/5
2		1/–					1/–
3		–/2	5/2				5/4
4			3/–	–/1			3/1
5			3/–	3/–			6/–
6			3/–	2/–	1/1		6/1
7		1/–	3/–	2/1			6/1
8		1/1	5/–		–/1		6/2
9			4/–	1/–	–/3		5/3
10			3/1	3/–	–/1		6/2
11					–/1		–/1
12		1/–	1/–		1/–		3/–
13		–/1	1/–	1/–	1/–		3/1
14							
15			–/1	1/–	1/1		2/2
16						–/1	–/1
17							
18					2/–		2/–
19							
20					–/3	–/1	–/4
21≤					–/2	–/2	–/4
Unknown		1/–					1/–
Total	3/1	9/4	31/7.0	13/3.0	0.6/13	–/4	62/32

Source: Questionnaire survey and interview survey
The figure indicates the number of staff in each category at studios with Japanese clients and studios with Western clients

3.4.1.2 Labor Supply Status

As for the final educational background of staff, university graduates form the largest group in the staff of both studios with Japanese clients and those with Western clients. Thirty-two of the 62 staff at studios with Japanese clients and 20 of the 32 staff at studios with Western clients were university graduates. In South Korea, a university offers a course related to animation production. However, as of 2014, there was no technical school that acts as a source of labor supply for the Japanese animation industry (see also Chap. 2). Twenty-two of the 32 university graduates at studios with Japanese clients and 11 of the 20 university graduates at studios with Western clients had been enrolled in a course related to animation production at university. Staff who completed the course had acquired basic skills before taking up employment. However, according to interviews with Studio M, new staff with only a high school qualification need to acquire skills on the production site after taking up employment because there is no technical school in South Korea. Staff with basic skills also need to train to enhance their skills after employment.

In relation to work experience, 30 of the 62 staff at studios with Japanese clients responded that they had worked in other industries. Of these, 20 responded "other," which indicated that many had moved from industries other than the related content industry. At studios with Western clients, 13 of the 32 staff had worked in other industries. Of these, six had moved from the related content industry. There were more staff from the related content industry in these studios compared with studios with Japanese clients.

Freelancers were asked why they had chosen their current form of employment. The most popular response of freelancers at studios with Japanese clients is "I can utilize my skills," provided by 40 of the 50 respondents, excluding those who did not respond, followed by positive responses such as "I do not want to be a regular employee" (25 respondents) and "I can choose my work" (12 respondents). Other responses were reasons such as "other" (13 respondents) and "no specific reason" (13 respondents). However, in many cases, such staff members appear to choose "work as a freelancer" because of their confidence in their own technical skills and a desire to be free to choose their work.

The most popular response from freelancers working for studios with Western clients is "I can utilize my skills," provided by 11 of the 18 respondents, followed by "there are few time constraints" (seven respondents), "I can choose my work" (five respondents), "no specific reason" (four respondents), and "the intentions of the studio with which I am associated" (three respondents). As with freelancers at studios with Japanese clients, confidence in their own technical skills and the desire to be free are considered to be important.

Studios were asked about their criteria when hiring staff. Four of the six studios with Japanese clients responded "motivation toward work," "work experience in the animation industry," and "skills above a specific level." The other response was "able to meet deadlines." According to Studio C, the initial criteria when hiring a staff member is the type of production in which the candidate had garnered experience. An assessment then took place of the technical skills by asking the candidate to draw a picture. Candidates with no track record in the animation industry were given a trial period of approximately 3 months, during which they received technical guidance. Also, social skills such as communication ability and cooperation were deemed to be secondary. Studios with Japanese clients focused on the technical criteria of a staff member's productive capacity.

In contrast, five of the seven studios with Western clients responded "skills above a specific level." Other responses were "motivation toward work" (four studios) and "work experience in the animation industry" (three studios). Such studios also cited responses that were not mentioned by studios with Japanese clients, such as "originality" (three studios), "cooperation to work in a team" (two studios), and "communication skills" (one studio). Studios with Western clients also emphasized creative aspects in addition to technical aspects. In this way, the important aspects differ between studios with Japanese clients and those with Western clients when hiring staff.

Staff moved freely between studios with Japanese clients and those with Western clients for production studios until around 2000. However, there has been no such exchange in recent years, according to Studio O. The reason for this change was that from around 2000, some production studios started receiving foreign orders for storyboard and layout work, both of which properly belong in a creative depart-ment. There are also differences between Japan and the West regarding market expectations of the feature of products such as storylines and expression. As a result of the addition of creative department processes to sole production department pro-cesses borne by the South Korean animation industry, differences in the feature of product and preference of markets in major client countries have complicated mobility for staff.

Incidentally, these differences were reflected in the working space of studios. There are many computers for digitalizing graphics in studios with Western clients. However, there more drawing boards and paper for key pictures and animation pic-tures in studios with Japanese clients (Figs. 3.5 and 3.6).

Fig. 3.6 Workspace in a studio with western clients (2006). *Note*: The studio workspace is divided by partitions and each cubicle has a computer

3.4.2   Social Relationships of Staff

3.4.2.1   Opportunities for Staff to Acquire Technical Skills

To our inquiries concerning the available opportunities to acquire technical skills, staff at studios with Japanese clients most often reported "guidance on the job from senior staff members" (39 of the 62 respondents), followed by "acquiring skills at educational establishments" (18 respondents). For staff at studios with Western clients, the most popular response was also "guidance on the job from senior staff members" (14 of the 32 respondents), followed by "acquiring skills through self-education after joining the industry" (11 respondents) and "acquiring skills at educational establishments" (11 respondents).

As these findings indicate, for both categories, technical skills were mostly acquired on the job under the guidance of senior staff. Freelancers in particular tended to gain opportunities for acquiring technical skills through work. Thirty-two freelancers (64 %) at studios with Japanese clients and 14 freelancers (73 %) at studios with Western clients stated that they received "guidance on the job from senior staff." Furthermore, in animation production, the methods of acquiring skills also differ, given that the technical skills to be acquired differ according to the processes involved. Staff at studios with Western clients embrace a greater variety of opportunities to acquire skills compared with staff at studios with Japanese clients. Many staff at studios with Western clients perform multiple types of work. These staff members seek out opportunities in line with their acquired technical skills.

3.4.2.2   Opportunities for Staff to Obtain Work

Table 3.9 presents the results of the survey of the work situation of staff during 1 month. Only eight of the 62 staff (two regular employees, four freelancers, and two with other or unknown status) at studios with Japanese clients responded that they

Table 3.9 Number of work referral contacts

Number of contacts (person)	Studios with Japanese clients				Studios with Western clients			
	Regular workers	Freelances	Others	Total	Regular workers	Freelances	Others	Total
0	2	39	–	41	3	7	1	11
1	1	8	1	10	–	5	–	5
2	3	3		3	2	3	1	6
3	–	–	1	3	2	1	–	3
4	–	–	–	–	–	1	–	1
5≤	1	1	1	2	2	1	1	4
Unknown	2	2	–	3	–	1	1	2
Total	6	53	3	62	9	19	4	32

Source: Questionnaire survey and interview survey

had multiple contacts who could act as intermediaries for obtaining their work (hereafter, work referral contacts). This indicates that the majority of staff at studios with Japanese clients were devoted to the work of the studio to which they are affiliated. However, 53 of the 62 staff at studios with Japanese clients were involved in a number of products per month. This finding suggests that these staff members were attempting to increase their earnings by increasing their manageable workload through specialization in a specific job category. In contrast, roughly 40 % of respondents (six regular employees, six freelancers, two with other or unknown status) at studios with Western clients had received referrals for work from multiple friends or acquaintances. Staff at studios with Western clients promote themselves relatively freely and do not restrict themselves to the studios to which they are affiliated.

According to Studio L, a studio can maintain a high level of product quality by taking on technically skilled staff as regular employees. Also, such regular employees received work requests on the basis of their individual capabilities. The reputation that technically skilled employees enjoy with other studios could enhance the studio's own technical reputation. For this reason, studios tacitly approve such employees' involvement in the work of other studios as long as the additional work does not impede the employees' performance in their studio.

3.4.2.3   Reasons for Continuing to Work in Seoul

Studio staff gave their reasons for why they continued to work in Seoul. The main responses from staff at studios with Japanese clients covered issues relating to proximity to the workplace, such as "large number of production studios" (50 respondents), "convenient transportation" (39 respondents), and easy access to information within the industry ("ease of obtaining inside industry information," 29 respondents). Concerning access to information, responses also included the existence of specific staff members ("Presence of person I want to work with," 18 respondents) and the existence of opportunities to acquire technical skills and work referral contacts ("large number of colleagues," 14 respondents). In other words, in addition to proximity to the industry, staff at studios with Japanese clients were also mindful of their relationships with their colleagues. In particular, this tendency was noticeable among freelancers compared with regular employees.

For staff at studios with Western clients, 26 of the 32 staff indicated that the "large number of production studios" in Seoul was important. Other responses included "convenient transportation" (16 respondents), "ease of obtaining inside industry information" (ten respondents), and "large number of colleagues" (ten respondents). These findings suggest that staff at studios with Western clients also focused on proximity to the industry. Only four staff members indicated the importance of the "presence of person I want to work with." Regular employees focused on the easy access to "information, in addition to large number of production studios." Many freelancers responded that they focused on relationships with other staff members. Concerning the type of work performed by staff, many respondents were involved in the animation picture process. This process tends to entail low job security and low income. As mentioned earlier, staff at studios with Western clients promoted themselves freely compared with staff at studios with Japanese clients. This finding indicates that freelancers with low job security and involved in the lower process are avoiding income insecurity by finding work outside of their affiliated studio through their relationships with other staff members.

In this way, by expanding their connections in Seoul, staff in both categories, but mainly freelancers, offer production studios an expert and flexible labor force.

3.5 Conclusion

Based on the results of the examination discussed above, Fig. 3.7 presents the agglomeration structure of the animation industry in Seoul. The South Korean animation industry has developed based on the international division of labor in relation to Japan and the West. The domestic market is modest in size, and the sales rely

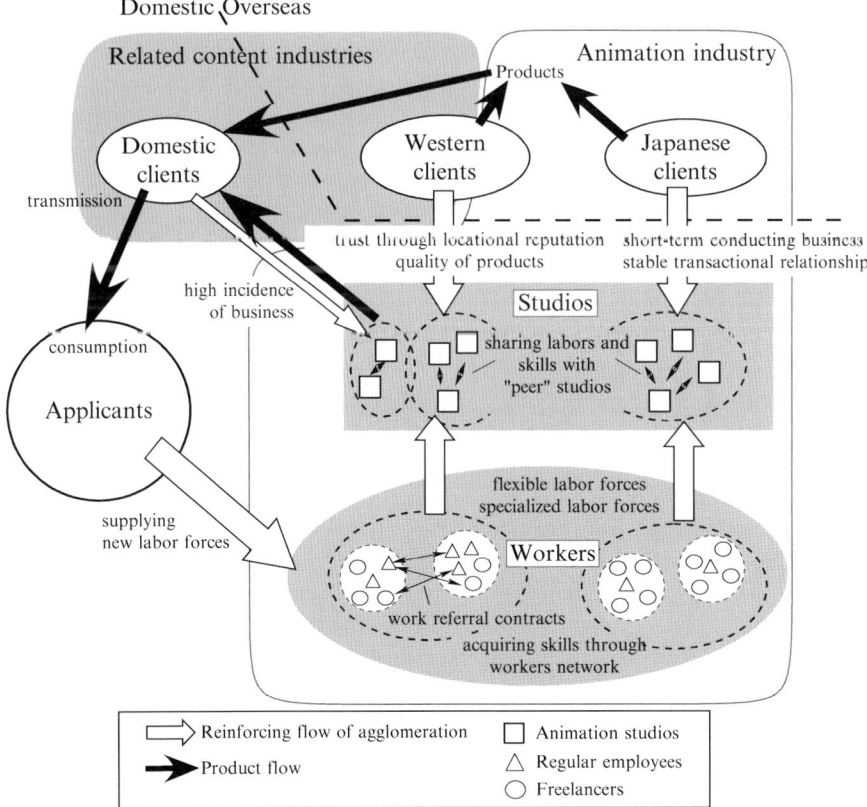

Fig. 3.7 Agglomeration structure model of the animation industry in Seoul

on subcontracting from foreign production companies. Seventy-four percent of production studios are located within Seoul. The characteristics of this industry in South Korea are multifaceted because of differences in the major client countries. However, location in the metropolis is considered essential for the studios regardless of their features. At the same time, there are differences in the preferred location within the city. Focusing on production studios and workers as the principal participants, we discuss below the reasons why the animation industry agglomerates in Seoul based on the specific features of the participants' activities and the relationship among the participants.

The principal clients of studios that mainly conduct business with Japan (i.e., studios with Japanese clients) specialize in animation production as business activity. Proximity to other studios in the same industry for sharing labor and proximity to the international airport to facilitate frequent business with Japanese studios were sought. Production studios locate themselves in Seoul to satisfy these conditions.

Studio staff have diverse educational backgrounds and professional experience. There are many freelancers. Staff acquire technical skills on the job under the guidance of senior staff. Staff members are affiliated to a specific production studio and rely on that studio for most of their work. Production studios focus on technical skills when employing staff. Staff members plan to increase viable production volumes by polishing their specific occupational skills to secure their employment. Staff members at studios with Japanese clients remain in Seoul to work by seeking proximity to the industry and contact with colleagues. This pool of staff offers a flexible and expert workforce to studios with Japanese clients.

In contrast, the principal clients of studios that conduct business with the West (i.e., studios with Western clients) and studios operating mainly in the domestic market (i.e., studios with domestic clients) operate in the related content industry in addition to animation production. Studios locate themselves in Seoul, particularly in the CBD, to gain proximity to other studios in the same business in order to share labor and skills, and seek improvement in their credibility and accessibility to the international airport.

At studios with Western clients, many freelancers are employed, which is the same for staff at studios with Japanese clients. Staff members select various opportunities to acquire technical skills following employment according to the type of work they perform. Studios focus on creative aspects in addition to technical aspects when employing staff. Some staff members are permitted to promote themselves relatively freely and are involved in production outside the studios to which they are affiliated. Proximity to the industry is considered important by staff at studios with Western clients for continuing to work in Seoul. Also, staff, freelancers in particular, who are in charge of lower process, consider contacts with professional colleagues as important for obtaining work. A structure that supplies a flexible and expert workforce based on the connection among staff has been formed for the pool of staff at studios with Western clients.

References

Association of Japanese Animations (2012) Anime Sangyo Repoto 2012 [Report of animation industry 2012] The Association of Japanese Animations, Tokyo (Japanese)

Korea Creative & Content Agency (2010) Daehanmingook Aenimeisyeon Saneop Baekseo [Korea animation industry white paper 2010]. Korea Culture & Contents Agency, Seoul (Korean)

Korea Culture & Contents Agency (2004) Daehanmingook Aenimeisyeon Saneop Baekseo [Korea animation industry white paper 2004]. Korea Culture & Contents Agency, Seoul (Korean)

Korea Culture & Contents Agency (2005) Daehanmingook Aenimeisyeon Saneop Baekseo [Korea animation industry white paper 2005]. Korea Culture & Contents Agency, Seoul (Korean)

Japan External Trade Organization (2007) Kankoku niokeru Kontentsu Sangyou no Jittai [The real form of content industry in Korea]. The Japan External Trade Organization Web site http://www3.jetro.go.jp/jetro-file/BodyUrlPdfDown.do?bodyurlpdf=05001428_001_BUP_0.pdf. Accessed 3 July 2008 (Japanese)

Kim H (2001) Gooknae Aenimeisyeon ui Giheok Jejak Sisutem Modele kwanhan Yeongoo [The study of animation planning and production in Korea]. Rep Korean Film Coun 2001–9:30–38 (Korean)

Lent JA (1998) The animation industry and its offshore factories. In: Sussman G, Lent JA (eds) Global productions. Hampton Press, Inc., Cresskill

Chapter 4
Agglomeration of the Animation Industry in the Shanghai–Wuxi Region, China

Abstract This chapter examines the agglomeration structure of the Chinese animation industry in Shanghai and Wuxi, two industrial cities located in the Yangtze Delta region. Like the South Korean animation industry, the Chinese animation industry has developed as a subcontracting industry that serves other countries. The focus of the investigation in this chapter includes the transactional relationships among studios and the combined labor market formed in the two cities. China's agglomeration structure is different from that of South Korea because of aspects such as state involvement in development and industrial distribution, the size of the domestic market, and the role the industry plays within the international division of labor. The productivity of the animation studios in the Shanghai–Wuxi region is also sustained by transactional relationships, which help to ensure that complementary skills and labor are mutually dispersed among studios. Workers in Shanghai find work and learn skills through their personal networks. Wuxi is a major investment city in China because of its industrial promotion policies and its moderate labor regulations. Each worker in Wuxi receives work only from the studio to which he or she belongs. The two cities have different agglomeration structures, but certain factors promote the industry's agglomeration in both cities.

Keywords China • Governmental policies • International division of labor • Labor market • Shanghai • Transactional relationships • Wuxi

4.1 Introduction

This chapter examines the development of the animation industry and its agglomeration structure in the Shanghai region, China. The history of Chinese animation production can be traced back to the 1920s. However, the modern animation industry started in the 1990s, adopting the animation picture and coloring processes of the Japanese and Western animation industries. In this respect, the animation industry in China has a commonality with that in Seoul, South Korea. However, its agglomeration structure differs from that in South Korea in aspects such as the state

© Springer Japan 2014

K. Yamamoto, *The Agglomeration of the Animation Industry in East Asia*,
International Perspectives in Geography: AJG Library 4,
DOI 10.1007/978-4-431-55093-8_4

involvement in the development and location of the industry, size of the domestic market, and the role it plays within the international division of labor.

Interviews were conducted with studio managers in Shanghai and Wuxi, which is located approximately 160 km west of Shanghai, one of the industrial cities in the Yangtze delta region, and staff were surveyed with a questionnaire. The interviews were conducted with nine studios located in Shanghai in August 2007 (six studios) and June 2008 (three studios). In addition, a written response was received from one studio in June 2008. Furthermore, we approached studios located in Wuxi introduced by Japanese production studios in their surveys from September 2006, July 2008, and August 2008. As a result, a face-to-face interview was conducted for one studio (2006), a written response was received from one studio (2008), and a response was received from one studio through staff in charge of the Japanese production studios (2008).[1]

4.2   State of Development of the Chinese Animation Industry

4.2.1   Structure of the Animation Market in China

The total income of all of China's broadcasting entities for 2006 was 38,655,114,000 yuan,[2] of which Shanghai accounted for 8,498,238,000 yuan (21.9 %) (Fig. 4.1). The income of Shanghai's broadcasting entities was more than twice that of organizations controlled directly by the State Administration of Radio Film and Television (SARFT) (4,095,062,000 yuan)[3] and Zhejiang Province (3,719,186,000 yuan). Similarly, the industry's total profit was 3,530,749,000 yuan, of which Shanghai accounted for 937,061,000 yuan (26.5 %), followed by Beijing (633,168,000 yuan; 17.9 %) and Hunan Province (243,715,000 yuan; 6.9 %). These findings show that Shanghai's status is high in the country's broadcasting industry.

---

[1] In the studio surveys, there were some issues regarding the representativeness of the data, such as the significant gaps (a maximum of nearly 2 years) in the timing between the surveys, the small sample number of 13 studios, and the fact that studios that had links with foreign studios were mainly targeted to clarity the impact of foreign business in the Chinese animation industry. Nevertheless, it seems that the survey results provide a general view of the industry as a whole, given the diverse attributes of the studios surveyed in Shanghai as indicated in Tables 4.1 and 4.2. Furthermore, the studios in Wuxi were all established to provide production service for Japanese production studios. The survey did not include studios in Wuxi that relied on other foreign markets or the domestic market. Therefore, this analysis is not intended to represent the Wuxi animation industry. Nevertheless, the survey results are still a useful source of information for examining the factors underlying the industry's agglomeration in the Shanghai region.

[2] 1 yuan = 15.55 yen or 0.1284 US dollars as of end of January 2007.

[3] SARFT is a body of the State Council of the People's Republic of China and is supervised by the Propaganda Department of the Communist Party of China Central Committee. It is a body that supervises and manages the media, including film, television, and radio.

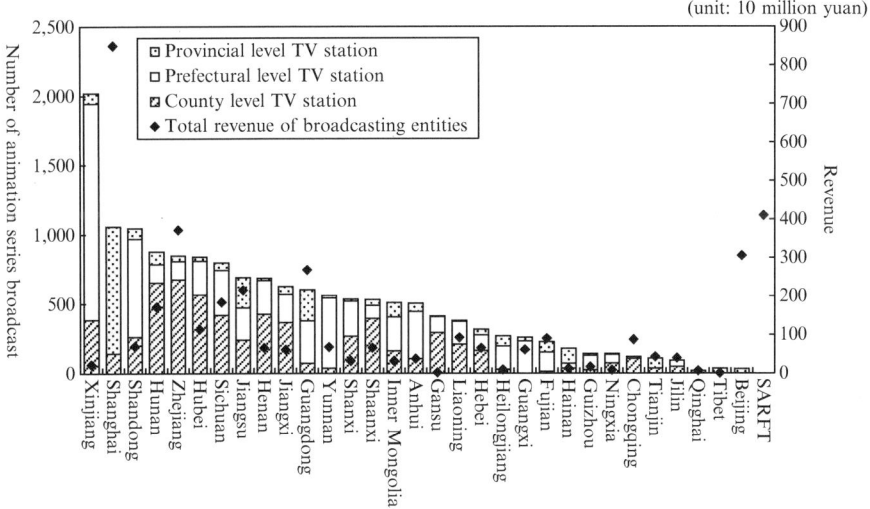

Fig. 4.1 Number of Animation Series Broadcast and Revenue Obtained by Chinese TV Stations (2006). *Note*: SARFT is State Administration of Radio, Film, and Television. *Source*: Based on "China Statistical Yearbook 2007"

The number of animation series aired by China's TV stations in 2006 is described as follows. In terms of the number of animation series aired, Shanghai ranked second among the nation's provinces, direct-controlled municipalities, and autonomous administrative divisions. However, in the scope of comparatively large province-level TV stations, Shanghai topped the list with 916 of the total 2,565 products aired.

Shanghai is thus China's most significant region in terms of animation products aired. However, it is the foreign rather than the domestic market that supports Shanghai's animation industry. Moreover, many of the products circulating in the domestic market are produced by foreign production studios, in particular, Japan. For example, according to the SARFT Development Research Center (2006), the government considers the animation industry as "a knowledge-, labor-, and technology-intensive cultural industry" (p. 177). At the same time, according to the Editorial Board of China Animation Yearbook (2006), the industry in China was "still in the early stages of development" (pp. 28–29), ranking it as a manual laborer subcontracted by animation superpowers such as Japan, South Korea, and the United States. Furthermore, according to the SARFT Development Research Center (2006), the volume of Chinese-made animation produced in 2005 was around 43,000 min compared with around 30,000 min subcontracted from foreign production studios. In addition, according to Qin (2006), of the top 15 animation series aired in China in 2004, 10 were Japanese-made.

4.2.2 Chinese Government Policy and Location of Studios

According to Zhang (2006), the Chinese government has increased its expectations of the animation industry since 1995. The government developed the domestic animation market by establishing various policies such as industry incentives and broadcasting regulations. Since then, as of 2014, the Chinese animation industry had been in a period of promoting efforts.

SARFT requires each TV station to allocate at least 60 % of animation airtime to domestic animation. Moreover, as an industrial growth policy in regional cities, it selects state level industrial base from the nation's studios, organizations, and industrial complexes, and encourages animation production. Some regional governments that own these industrial bases enforce their own policies of preferential treatment.[4]

From a review of the distribution (Fig. 4.2) of the 215 organizations and studios[5] that submitted applications for the production of animation[6] for the domestic market between 2004 and 2006, concentrations can be observed in Beijing (39 cases), Shanghai (27 cases), and Guangzhou (27 cases). Of the 39 cases in Beijing, 27 cases are directly controlled by the state and one by the Chinese People's Liberation Army. Excluding these 28 cases, there are 11 privately owned studios located in Beijing. In the case of Shanghai and Guangzhou, a concentration was also identified for animation production studios that had not applied to produce animation for the domestic market between 2004 and 2006. A search for the number of studios under the headings "film and television" and "film and TV production" on the online phone directory "Locoso"[7] using the keywords "animation production" shows concentrations in Wuxi (11 studios), Shanghai (nine studios), Hangzhou City (five studios), Zhengzhou City (four studios), and Wuhan City (three studios).[8] Many of these cities enforce preferential treatment policies, which confirms the effectiveness of the government's incentives policy.

---

[4] A review of the recent changes in broadcasting regulations made by the SARFT reveals that, in issuing its "Notice on additional regulations on supervising TV animation broadcasts" in August 2006, it prohibited TV stations from airing foreign products between 5 p.m. and 8 p.m. starting September 1 of that year. In its "Notice on reinforcing the supervision of TV animation broadcasts" issued on February 14, 2008, SARFT then also prohibited airing between 5 p.m. and 9 p.m. not only of foreign products, but also of programs introducing such products starting on May 1 of that year. On October 12, 2009, SARFT extended the ban on airing foreign products until 10 p.m. through its "Notice on further reinforcement of the supervision of TV animation broadcasts." In this way, regulations on any airing of foreign products during prime time have been in effect since 2006. At present, it has become difficult to view foreign animation during prime time. As a result, the production volume of domestic animation has been increasing in recent years to fill this lack of animation content. According to Lu (2011), the production volume of domestic TV animation was 21,819 min (29 series) in 2004 and 220,529 min (385 series) in 2010, representing a more than tenfold increase in just 6 years.

[5] Aggregated by the author using the China Animation Yearbook 2006 for data.

[6] Under the Chinese broadcasting system, studios have to obtain permission to make new animation products by applying to the government with their project plans.

[7] China Telecom Group Yellow Pages Information Co., Ltd. (2008): Locoso (http://www.locoso.com/, last accessed on November 6, 2008)

[8] Both "film and television" or "film and TV production" here mean the production business of films or TV programs.

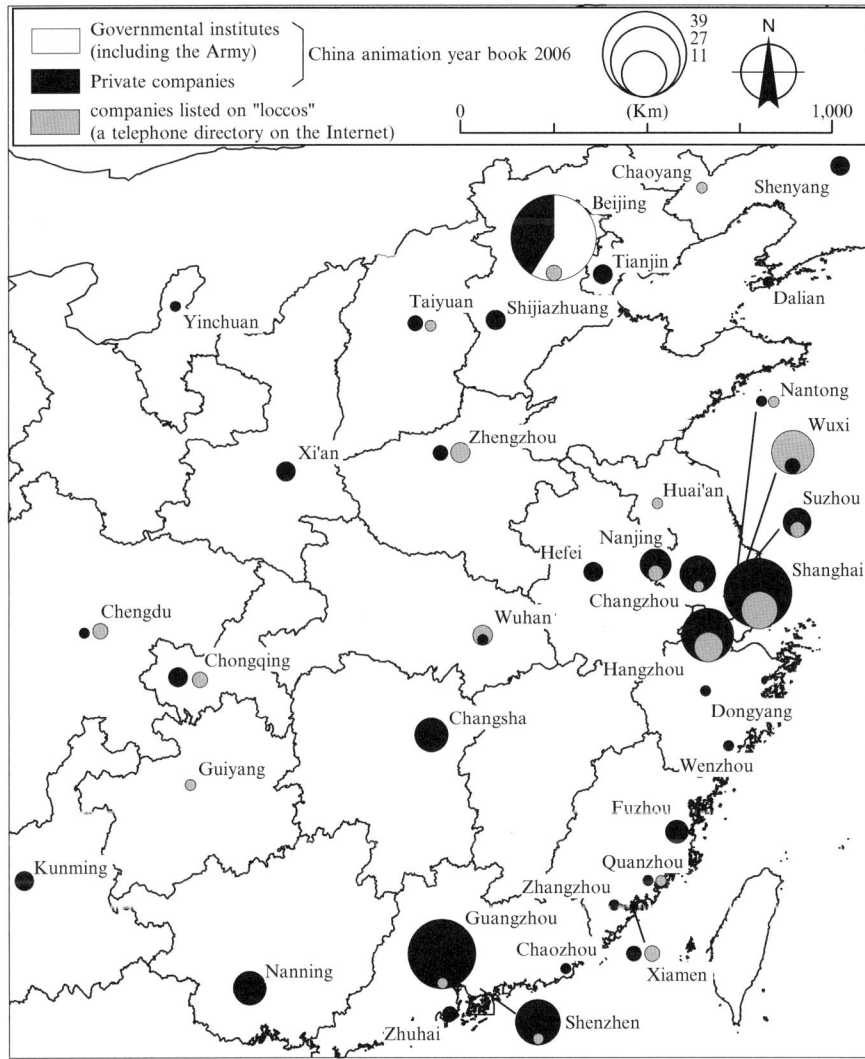

Fig. 4.2 Location of Animation Production Firms in China. *Source*: Based on "China Animation Yearbook 2006" and "locos," a telephone directory on the Internet

4.2.3 Positioning of the Shanghai Region

Wuxi is noticeable for the ratio between the number of studios appearing in Locoso on one hand and the China Animation Yearbook 2006 on the other. The impact of conducting business with foreign production studios, Japanese production studios in particular, may explain the trend in the establishment of production studios in Wuxi.

At the time of the survey, although the Chinese animation industry had a huge potential domestic market, the overseas markets support the industry. As mentioned earlier, Japanese animation, studios are their major clients. Joint delivery methods such as association delivery and professional delivery are used for Japanese orders placed with Chinese production studios.[9] There is currently one flight that operates an association delivery and another that operates a professional delivery. The schedules for association delivery and professional delivery between Japan and China are adjusted frequently and shipments take place almost every day. More than ten Japanese production studios participate in association delivery. Four out of the nine Chinese studios that used association delivery in March 2008 were located in Shanghai. Furthermore, three studios were located in Wuxi and one studio each in Hangzhou and Jiaxing cities. In addition, professional delivery was used by one studio in Wuxi. In addition, of the 11 production studios in Wuxi, as shown in Fig. 4.2, five conducted business with Japanese production studios. Together with Shanghai, Wuxi was a major Chinese city in the division of labor for Japanese animation production studios.

Thus, on the basis of product supply to domestic market and international business, the Shanghai region, including Wuxi, is a region where the animation industry has agglomerated in China. The analysis below deals with the Shanghai region, Shanghai and Wuxi in particular, because Shanghai is located at the center of the agglomeration and Wuxi is noticeable for its special features in conducting business with Japan.

4.3   Features of Business Between Studios

4.3.1   Location of Studios in Cities

Before our close analysis, here we discuss the location of production studios in Shanghai and Wuxi. Figure 4.3 shows the distribution of studios within the city of Shanghai based on the data provided by the China Animation Association. The data show that studios are widely distributed in the city, with a concentration along the western stretch of the inner ring road.[10] This area is home to the Shanghai Animation Film Studio, which has led the Chinese animation industry. Furthermore, Studio α was located in the vicinity. Studio α was established in 1989 with full Taiwanese capital as the first domestic production studio that specialized in foreign

---

[9] See Chaps. 2 and 3 for further discussions on association delivery and professional delivery.

[10] Shanghai's urban area is roughly divided by the inner and outer ring roads. The inner ring road comprises Zhongshan, Longyang, Luoshan, Ningguo, and Huangxing roads, and the outer ring road comprises the A20 Highway. The inner ring road area is positioned as the center of economic development, while the area between the inner and outer ring roads is residential districts. Furthermore, developing suburbs sprawl beyond the outer ring road.

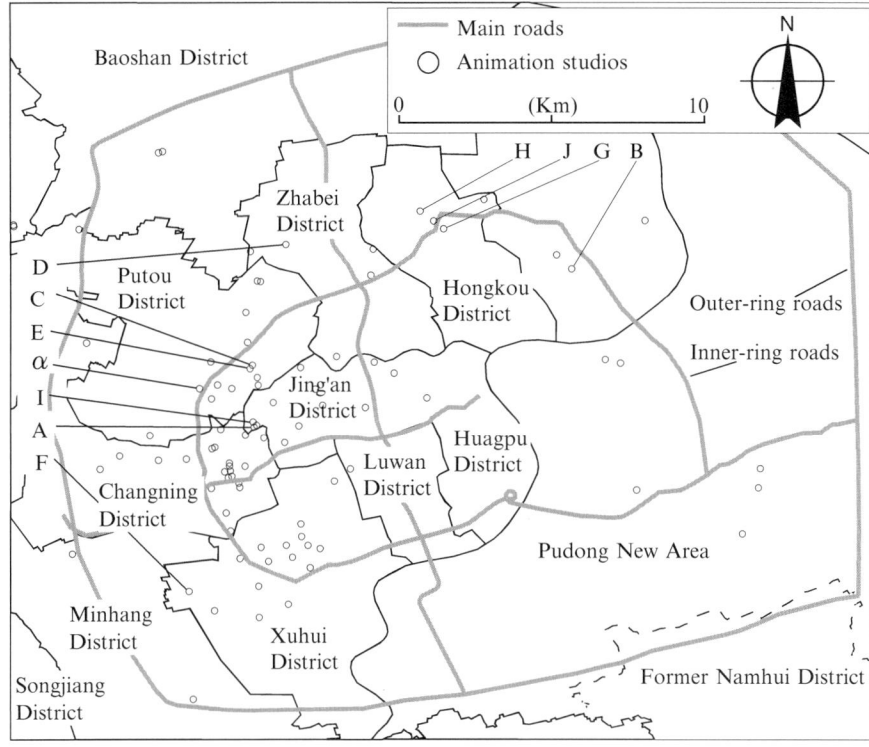

Fig. 4.3 Location of Animation Studios, Participating Studios, and Studio α. *Source*: Based on data provided by the Animation Association and interview survey

subcontracting.[11] Studio α withdrew from China in 2001, but studios derived from this studio are contributing to the growth of the animation industry in this area. Furthermore, there were only six studios located in Pudong Ward, a district designated for cultural industry promotion by the Shanghai municipal government.[12]

Figure 4.4 shows the location of the studios within Wuxi. Excluding the two studios located outside the area shown in the figure, all are located within

---

[11] According to the interview survey, the studio that established Studio α was an animation subcontractor in Taiwan that mainly serviced Japanese and US clients. Its founder came from a Taiwanese animation production studio.

[12] The report, "Some (preliminary) opinions on supporting the cultural development of Shanghai's Pudong Ward," issued by the Shanghai municipal government in August 2005 is a policy related to developing the animation industry (China Animation Yearbook 2006). According to this document, studios located in this area producing cultural products are given preferential treatment business-wise compared with other areas. At the same time, although this area was developed recently, it still does not match the city center in terms of proximity to other studios in the same or related industries, or in terms of the infrastructure maintenance of the surrounding areas. For these reasons, production studios often do not choose this location.

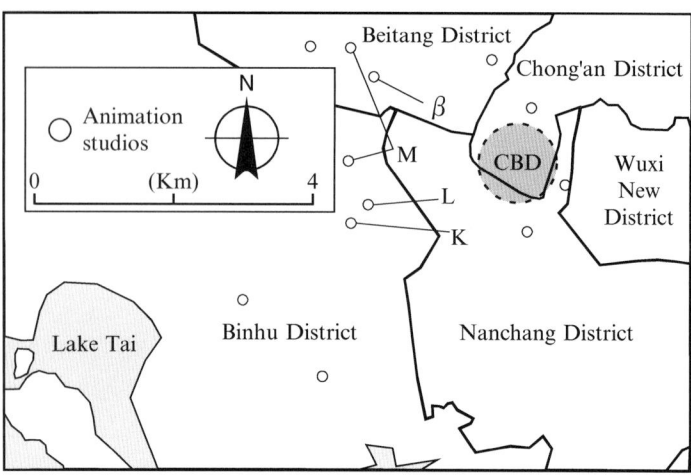

Fig. 4.4 Location of Animation Studios, Participating Studios, and Studio β in Wuxi. Studio M has two working places. *Source*: "Locos" a telephone directory on the Internet and interview survey

approximately 5 km from the city center.[13] Both studios are located in a new industrial complex zone. The studios tend to be distributed in the western parts of the city.

4.3.2 Attributes of Studios Surveyed

Table 4.1 summarizes the studios surveyed by year of establishment per city.[14] The attributes of each studio are discussed.

4.3.2.1 Basic Production Studio Attributes

First, in relation to the basic attributes of production studios located in Shanghai, Studio A was the first to be established (1957) and had the largest capital with 18,830,000 yuan. It was followed by Studio F with 5,000,000 yuan and Studio D with 3,000,000 yuan (Table 4.1). In general, studios established before 2000 tended to have a larger capital compared with those established later. Similarly, in terms of

---

[13] These sites are located on the outskirts of Wuxi, approximately 20 min by car to the southeast of the city center. Wuxi's municipal plan (2001–2020) earmarked this area for comprehensive logistics-oriented development centered on the outward-looking economy and the high-tech industry. These two studios receive preferential treatment, as they fulfill the conditions set forth in Wuxi's policy to promote the animation industry, which is presented in footnote 18.

[14] Written responses were received from Studios I and K.

Table 4.1 Basic Attributes of Participating Studios

Cities	Studios	Year of establishment	Capital (Unit: 10,000 yuan)	Number of employees	Annual sales	Productivity	Origin of establishment	Year of survey held
Shanghai	A	1957	1,883	200+	2,010	×	State-owned	2007
	B	Late 1970	140	60+	×	750	Foreign-subcontracting	2007
	C	1994	150	50+	×	528	Foreign-funded (USA)	2007
	D	1998	300	130+	×	×	Foreign-subcontracting	2007
	E	1998	50	74+	600	×	Spin-off (E)	2007
	F	1998	500	100+	500	×	Foreign-funded (Taiwan)	2007
	G	2001	×	25+	×	240	Spin-off (α)	2008
	H	2003	50	30+	×	400	Spin-off (A)	2008
	I	2004	50	42+	×	×	Expansion	2008
	J	2006	80	40+	×	500	Spin-off (α)	2008
Wuxi	K	2001	54	113+	187	×	Foreign-funded (Japan)	2008
	L	2002	10	120+	×	1,875	Foreign-funded (Japan)	2006
	M	2005	40	120+	×	750	Spin-off (β)	2008

Source: Interview survey

The year of establishment is based on establishment at current location

The annuals sales reported for Studio A represents only its sales to its biggest client

"+" after the number of employees means that the studio hires varying numbers of freelancers as necessary

"×" indicates unknown/not disclosed

Productivity is measured in broadcast minutes allotted to the animated films produced by each studio. In the interview survey, Studios B, L, and M did provide this data, but provided the number of animation pictures they had produced. From there, productivity was estimated as the number of pictures produced divided by (8×60), as most Japanese animated films are broadcast at eight pictures per a second

Formula: the number of animation pictures produced ÷ 8 (the number of frames in a second) ÷ 60 (seconds)

employee numbers, many of the studios established after 2000 were small in scale.[15] The studios surveyed were characterized as able to produce 2D digital animation and 3D computer graphic animation (studios A, C, D, F, I), limited to specific processes in 2D animation (B, E, G), limited to specific processes in 3D computer graphic animation (H), and unknown (J). Furthermore, the major client countries (Table 4.2) were Japan (B, F), the United States (F, I, J), and France (C, D, E, H). Some studios conducted business with multiple countries (C, F, J). As the Editorial Board of China Animation Yearbook (2006) indicates, the Chinese animation industry performs labor-intensive processes for foreign business. The orders from foreign studios show that all studios with such relationships specialized in the production department, except undisclosed ones. Excluding studios A, I, and G, business with foreign studios expressed as a percentage of total revenue (hereafter, foreign dependence ratio) is at least 50 %. As for domestic business, there were own product sales to domestic TV stations and the related content industry in addition to subcontracting from those in the same business category.

The studios can be grouped into the following five categories in relation to their establishment: (1) reorganized from a state organization into a state-owned studio (A) (hereafter, state-owned-type); (2) established with the aim of subcontracting from foreign production studios (B, D) (hereafter, foreign-subcontracting-type); (3) established with funds from foreign production studios (C, F) (hereafter, foreign-funded-type); (4) spun off from existing animation production studios (E, G, H, J) (hereafter, spin-off-type); and (5) established by domestic companies in other industries with the aim of developing new business (I) (hereafter, expansion-type).

Of these types, Studio A is one of the largest domestic studios designated as a part of the state-level industrial base. With the aim of creating an animation industry, it was the first animation production studio to be established in China and played a pioneering role in establishing the industry. Today, it has been reorganized from a state organization into a state-owned studio. Studio B was established by its owner based on the knowledge and personal connections he gained while helping establish Studio α. Upon Studio α's withdrawal from China, Studio B took over Studio α's name and part of its business activities in China. Studio C's head office is in Hong Kong. Its animation production is shared between Shanghai and group studios in Changzhou and Hangzhou cities. As with Studio C, Studio F also shares production work with group studios at two domestic locations (Nanjing and Suzhou cities). Studio I was established in 2004 as a studio affiliated with a toy manufacturer in Suzhou City. It entered the market through an expansion of its parent company's business.

The state-owned-, foreign-subcontracting-, and foreign-funded-type studios all had a capital of at least 1,400,000 yuan, which is larger in comparison with the spin-off-type studios (not more than 800,000 yuan) and the expansion-type studios (500,000 yuan). Regarding employee numbers, the state-owned-type studio had the

---

[15] Staff numbers fluctuated in many studios in line with press and slack business periods. Some studios responded that they added around 50 staff members during busy periods. This fact suggests that a flexible workforce exists.

Table 4.2 Business fields of foreign clients of participating studios

Cities	Studios	Dependency rate on foreign clients	Foreign conducted business			Subcontracted process										
			Countries or regions	Product category	Field	Planning	Directing	Rendering	Key picture	Animation picture	Coloring	Background	Shooting	Sound effect	Editing	Computer graphic
Shanghai	A	*	Southeast Asia	ORG	TV	–										
	B	100	Japan	OEM	An					o	o					
	C	75	France, Italy	OEM	An				o	o	o	o	o		o	o
	D	70–80	France	OEM	An	×										
	E	80	France	OEM	An				o	o						
	F	70	U.S., Japan, Europe	OEM	An	×										
	G	0	–	–	–	–										
	H	50	France	OEM	×	×			o	o	o					
	I	30	U.S.	OEM	An											
	J	60	U.S., Europe	OEM	×				o	o	o					
Wuxi	K	100	Japan	OEM	An				o	o	o					
	L	100	Japan	OEM	An				o	o	o					
	M	100	Japan	OEM	An				o	o	o					

Source: Interview survey

Dependency on foreign clients is calculated as sales from foreign clients divided by annual sales

Studio A's dependency rate on foreign clients is not unknown; the studio is mainly dependent on domestic transactions

Countries or regions indicate the countries or regions that each studio is primarily dependent on

In Product category: *ORG* studio's own products, *OEM* subcontracted products

In Field category: *An* animation production, *TV* TV broadcasting service

"–" indicates that this information was not requested in the survey

"×" indicates data unknown (including data not disclosed)

largest with "200 or more," significantly higher than that at spin-off-type studios (e.g., E, 74 employees) and the expansion-type studios (42 employees).

Next, the basic attributes of the three production studios located in Wuxi (hereafter, Wuxi production studios) will be compared with Shanghai. These studios' capital was small, no greater than 540,000 yuan (K). In contrast, all three studios had large employee numbers, with a minimum of 100. All surveyed studios were established after 2000. Business with Japanese production studios accounted for all of these studios' sales (Table 4.2) because Japanese production studios (K, L) and investors (M) were heavily involved in establishing the Wuxi production studios. Studios K and L were established as production departments of Japanese production studios and are classified as foreign-funded-type studios. Furthermore, though a spin-off studio, Studio M separated from Studio β and was established with financial support from Chinese investors living in Japan. Studio β was the first studio to be established in Wuxi with the aim of subcontracting from Japan. Its year of establishment is unknown. It was founded by a former staff member at Studio α in Shanghai, who took his colleagues with him. The founder was prompted to start his own studio after a shift in Studio α changed its management policy of mainly subcontracting from Western production studios.[16] Studio M works with production studios in Japan run by Chinese investors and receives orders exclusively from such production studios.

4.3.2.2 Reasons for Production Studio Location

First, the impact of the founding history of a studio on its choice of location will be examined (Figs. 4.3 and 4.4). In relation to Shanghai production studios, the foreign-subcontracting- and spin-off-type studios tend to locate themselves in the northern part of the city. Wuxi production studios, as spin-off-type studios, were located near their studio of origin (Studio β), while the foreign-funded-type studios tend to be located in the western part of the city. However, the special location characteristics within the city are not clear. Various reasons were given for studios' choice of location in any city. Some production studios moved frequently, for example, upon renewal of their 1-to-3 year rental agreements. The relationship between studio location and other attributes such as studio size, major client countries, and business content is unclear, for several possible reasons. Private land ownership is not approved in China. Government authorization is required to use land. The intentions of the government and the realtors who develop sites with government authorization significantly influence production studios' location decisions. Consequently, the

---

[16] Today, Studio β produces 150,000 animation pictures (or 312 min) per year and has around 300 staff. It is one of the largest studios located in Wuxi. It is assumed that among studios with Japanese clients in Wuxi, Studio β is pivotal because it was the first production studio to move into Wuxi, it is a Chinese studio that operated a professional delivery for a Japanese studio, Studio M was established as a spin-off studio from Studio β, and Studio K's interview responses.

Table 4.3 Reasons for site selection

Cities	Studios	Reasons
Shanghai	A	Controlling investment through the usage of the facilities of the film industry and expectation for synergy effect with the film market
	B	Ample labor supply. Good access to the international airport
	C	Ample labor supply with advanced techniques
	D	Ample labor supply. Good access to the international airport
	E	Rich human resources with techniques and easy to manage them
	F	Ample labor supply and lively place with the greatest economic development
	G	Rich qualified worker with high levels of cultural appreciation.
	H	The birthplace of the animation industry and developed industry with sophisticated culture
	I	Proximity to other studios and good transportation accessibility
	J	The birthplace of the animation industry and developed industry
Wuxi	K	Good access to the international airport and proximity to other studios
	L	Good access to the international airport and favorable governmental support and cheaper labor force than that of Shanghai
	M	Good access to the international airport. Loose restrictions over labor conditions than that in Shanghai. Human resources gathered through the connections of the founder. Labor force cheaper than that of Shanghai

Source: Interview survey

location of a production studio does not necessarily reflect the studio's own intentions adequately.

In exploring why each studio chose Shanghai or Wuxi as its location (Table 4.3), several tendencies could be observed depending on the chosen city and studio category. Of the Shanghai production studios, foreign-subcontracting- and foreign-funded-type studios seek proximity to foreign studios who are their major clients in terms of time ("good access to the international airport") and manpower for labor-intensive production activities ("ample labor supply").

As entities established with the aim of developing the domestic market or business expansion from other industries, the state-owned- and expansion-type studios appear to focus on controlling their initial investments by utilizing existing infrastructure, such as maintenance of the industrial infrastructures ("controlling investment through the usage of the facilities of the film industry") and better access to clients and other studios in the same industry ("expectation for synergy effect with the film market" and "good transportation accessibility").

The spin-off-type studios were established by staff members involved in specific processes. These studios tend to be relatively new and small. Such studios seek stable management by subcontracting from major studios. Consequently, it is considered that studios that have led the animation industry, such as Studios A, chose their locations based on the agglomeration of other studios in the same industry and the existence of highly skilled staff members.

Wuxi production studios cited the accessibility of and distance to the international airport. In other words, the accessibility of Shanghai Pudong International Airport, where association delivery and professional delivery were conducted, is the prerequisite for the location choice. Since these studios were established as production departments of Japanese production studios, they were expected to play this role and their major clients were limited to Japanese production studios. This is another important reason why Shanghai's foreign-subcontracting- and foreign-funded-type studios chose to locate in Shanghai.

Spin-off-type studios were able to use their founder's personal connections when established. According to Studio M, it was able to hire competent staff away from Studio β when it was established, which allowed it to maintain product quality from its inception.

The wage differential in Wuxi compared with Shanghai (L, M) and the lax controls on labor (M) were also pointed out. In relation to the wage differential, Studio L reported that it was easy to gather human resources in Wuxi since staff in the animation industry can be paid more compared with average staff members in Wuxi, while they are paid less compared with the staff members in the Shanghai animation industry. In addition, Studio M reported that Studio β chose Wuxi when it became independent because of rising wages in Shanghai and lax supervision of labor control in Wuxi. Business with Japan required working through the night because of tight production schedules and the local arrival time of half-finished products. However, there were strict controls on late-night work in Shanghai when Studio β was established. In contrast, these restrictions were lax in Wuxi and late-night work was tolerated (see also Figs. 4.5, 4.6 and Yamamoto 2012).

The proactive stance of the Wuxi municipal government to foster the animation industry has been the underlying cause of the lax controls on labor. For example, Studio L applied for authorization to establish itself with multiple local governments in the areas around Shanghai at the time of its establishment. Only Wuxi granted it authorization. In addition to preferential tax measures for foreign investment companies,[17] Wuxi also planned to implement a policy to promote the animation industry such as developing Wuxi National Animation Industrial Base (Fig. 4.7). Accordingly, expecting the application of both policies, the studio included Wuxi as a potential location.[18] However, Studio L could not meet the conditions for applica-

---

[17] Wuxi has implemented a preferential tax policy for foreign investment companies (http://qb.wuxi.gov.cn/web101/zcfg/wxs/103890.shtml last accessed on April 9th 2014).

[18] As a policy to promote the animation industry, Wuxi has issued the report "Some policy statements on encouraging and supporting the development of the animation/comics industry by the Wuxi municipal government" (2006). According to this provision, if a production company is located in the Wuxi National Animation Industry Base Zone and the Animation Industry Base Construction Guidance Team approves it as a "Wuxi Animation and Comic Industry Support Unit" (Article 1), or an animation production company with a good reputation domestically and overseas applies to move into the animation industry base and is approved as a "support unit" as defined above (Article 11), it can receive preferential treatment such as capital support (Articles 4 and 5), financing (Article 6, Paragraph 2), and financial incentives proportionate to production volume (Article 6, Paragraph 1). Companies located outside the zone can also receive one-off preferential

Fig. 4.5 Animation picture workspace in a Chinese production studio serving Japanese clients, Wuxi (2006). *Note*: Eighty workers produce animation pictures over the course of three consecutive work shifts each day in this workspace. *Source*: Yamamoto (2012b) Photo 6-1

tion from the industry promotion policy and only received preferential tax treatment targeted for foreign investment companies.

The above discussion demonstrates that the conditions set by a studio when choosing their location tend to differ depending on the city where the studio was located and the circumstances surrounding the studio's establishment. It seems that these conditions stem from business relationships with major clients expected at the time of establishment of the studio. For this reason, it is suggested that the circumstances surrounding a studio's establishment continue to affect the structure of its business following its establishment. Therefore, the business structure of studios is examined below in accordance with studio category by city.

---

treatment on the basis of deliberation by the guidance team if it has achieved prominent success in an area such as original animation (original film and TV animation) (Article 13). This scope of the provision was extended via an expansion notice (2007) to include production companies located outside the animation industry base as "companies related to the animation and comics industry," provided they were "particularly outstanding companies approved by the guidance team." Furthermore, the period during which a company can benefit from preferential treatment was increased from a one-off benefit to a permanent one (Article 4).

Fig. 4.6 Coloring workspace in a production studio serving Japanese clients (2006). *Note*: Animation pictures are digitalized by the scanner in the foreground. Workers color the scanned pictures over the course of three consecutive work shifts each day

4.3.3   *Characteristics of Production Studios' Business*

4.3.3.1   Business with Foreign Studios

Considering the focus of Shanghai production studios in relation to foreign business, foreign-funded-type Studio C cited grounds for domestic market activities in its business, the ability to gain dealership in the domestic market, and its high profitability. At the same time, the studio responded that it wished to avoid production solely for the domestic market because of the high managerial risk involved, the limited number of success stories in the domestic market, and an inadequate policy framework for copyright protection. Studio F responded that the work allowed it to enhance its technical skills through the studio's efforts because foreign studios require high product quality and the studio can then apply those high quality skills acquired through foreign business to produce its own material for the domestic market. They expect that if they are able to produce high-quality material, they will be better able to recover their capital investment even in the domestic market. These findings suggest that foreign-funded-type studios aim to move into the domestic market through their technical skills and capital acquired through foreign business.

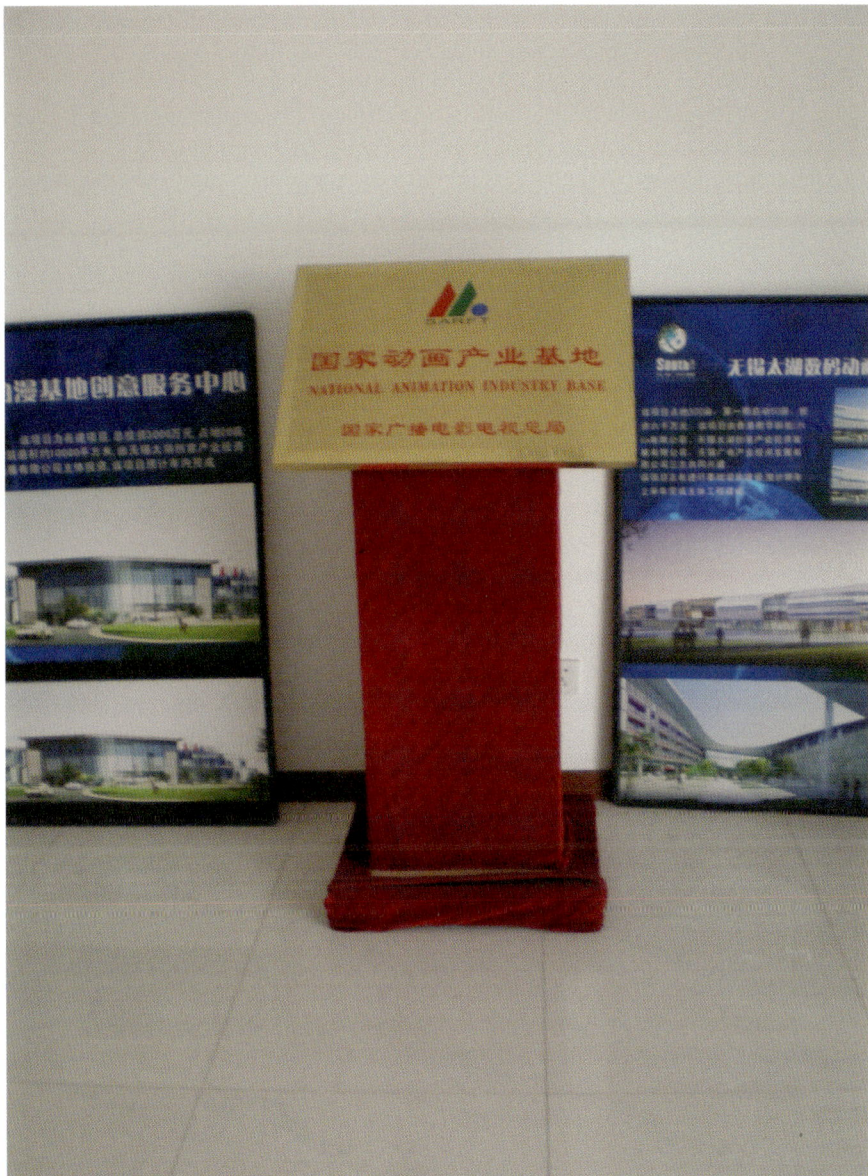

Fig. 4.7 Wuxi National Animation Industry Base (2006). *Note*: At the time of this investigation, this new urban area and its animation industry base were still under development

However, the spin-off-type studios' responses included trust based on payment (E, H) and sufficient technical skills ("the studio possesses the technical skills to meet client requirements") (J). These responses suggest the importance of trust in and by foreign studios, respectively. Studio B, a foreign-subcontracting-type studio, cited trust based on payment, which reflects the dependence of its operations on business with Japanese production studios. In addition to trust based on payment, Studio D cited the ability to gain dealership in the domestic market, indicating its intentions of domestic expansion using the dealership acquired through foreign business. No response was received from the expansion-type studio.

The government of Shanghai has a policy of supporting studio-targeted industrial development for the culture industry located in the city. According to this policy, up to the end of 2008, all companies in the culture industry located in the city were exempt from tax on income from orders by foreign companies and from corporate income tax. However, none of the studios cited this policy as a reason for conducting foreign business.

All Wuxi production studios cited "the intentions of the Japanese production studio" as a reason for conducting business with Japanese production studios. No business was undertaken apart from work through the Japanese production studios with which they had capital ties.[19]

4.3.3.2 Business with Domestic Studios

Product sales of the domestic business to the related content industry and work subcontracted from other studios in the same industry can be identified for the Shanghai production studios, but business with domestic studios cannot be identified for the Wuxi production studios (Table 4.4). The following subsections discuss the business conducted by the Shanghai production studios with domestic studios.

Studios' responses concerning clients, except undisclosed ones, included "TV stations, publishers, and toy manufacturers" (D), "publishers nearby" (H), Shanghai Media Group[20] (F), China Central Television (A, F, I), and Beijing Television (I). Direct sales of products to the related content industry and business with TV stations located in Beijing can be observed. According to Studio A, its staff frequently travel by plane to Beijing to meet with China Central Television staff. Studios conducting business with the related content industry can be observed in all categories. Business ties with other studios in the same industry can be observed in domestic business. Furthermore, Studio C suggests that the risks involved in recovering capital on products for the domestic market are avoided by conducting business with other studios in the same industry.

---

[19] According to interviews with the Japanese parent studios and affiliated studios, the aim of setting up a studio in Wuxi was to complement their own labor supply. The parent studio of studios K and L consider these studios as their production departments. Also, according to Studio M's affiliate, to secure stable production volume, the studio is prohibited from business other than that its affiliate studio arranges. This finding suggests that Japanese production studios significantly influenced the operations of the Wuxi studios.

[20] This is Shanghai's largest broadcasting entity, which includes Shanghai Television, Shanghai Oriental Television, and Shanghai Dragon Television.

Table 4.4 Business fields of domestic clients of participating studios

Cities	Studios	Domestic conducted business					
				Subcontracted process			
		Product category	Fields	Rendering	Key picture	Animation picture	Coloring
Shanghai	A	ORG	TV station	–			
	B	–	–	–			
	C	ORG	TV station	–			
	D	COL	TV station, Toy production, Publishing	–			
	E	OEM	Animation production	×			
	F	ORG	TV station	–			
	G	OEM	Animation production		o	o	
	H	OEM+ORG	Publishing	o	o	o	o
	I	OEM+ORG	Animation production, TV station	×			
	J	OEM+ORG	×		o	o	o
Wuxi	K	–	–	–			
	L	–	–	–			
	M	–	–	–			

Source: Interview survey
In Product category: ORG, studio's own products; OEM, subcontracted products
"–" indicates data not requested in the survey
"×" indicates data unknown (including data not disclosed)

Considering business with other studios in the same industry, the expansion-type studio conducted business with nearby Studio A. All the spin-off-type studios state they have business with "other studios in the same industry located nearby." Business with other studios in the same industry took shape through personal connections from the studio of origin, as noted by all spin-off-type studios (E, G, H, J).

For example, Studio E separated from Studio C in 1998, but Studio C is its largest client for domestic subcontract orders. According to Studio E, its owner used to work for Studio C, and thus is familiar with its internal affairs and payment system and has regular contact with Studio C's owner. For this reason, Studio C is considered a trustworthy studio with which Studio E continues to conduct business. Studio C contracts out parts of its production processes to five nearby production studios (including Studio E) as well as to group studios. All these five studios separated from Studio C. According to Studio C, it selected the five studios because of its knowledge of their technical skills base. The staff of these five studios have previously worked for Studio C, which results in trust. When placing an order, Studio C selects the studio with the best skills to match with the work requirements from these five studios. These findings suggest that ongoing contact fosters a relationship of trust between business partners. The subcontractor has the benefit of payment security and the client enjoys technical quality.

The founder of Studio G worked in animation picture process at Studio α and left that studio when it withdrew from the market. Since its inception, Studio G's business was limited to key picture and animation picture processes. According to Studio G, many production studios also separated from Studio α and located nearby to specialize in specific processes. Studio G maintains close ties with these "former colleagues" to supplement its technical skills base. One such studio acts as a negotiator in foreign business and production for the domestic market, and is in charge of allocating work.

A hierarchy is seen among the studios in this examination of the features of the foreign and domestic businesses. In other words, a group of relatively large studios aim to launch products for which they have dealership and copyright into the domestic market using capital, technical skills, and labor force. However, a group of small studios aim to achieve stable operation by establishing close business ties with large studios and other studios in the same industry located nearby to supplement their technical skills and labor force. Furthermore, mutual trust based on payment and technical skills is built between studios with close relationships, such as studios of origin and "former colleague" studios, which becomes the basis of business.

4.4 Characteristics of the Labor Market

As indicated in the reason of choice of location of production studios, skilled staff are living in the Shanghai region. In this section, the characteristics of staff members in the animation industry are examined based on a questionnaire survey conducted among staff at Shanghai and Wuxi studios. From studios willing to cooperate in the survey, 58 staff at five studios in Shanghai (A, 14; B, 5; C, 23; E, 5; F, 11) (hereafter, Shanghai production studio staff) responded in August 2007. Similarly, responses were received from 53 staff affiliated with one Wuxi production studio (M) (hereafter, Wuxi production studio staff) in October 2007. As only one production studio was surveyed in Wuxi and the survey took place before the new Labor Contract Law of the People's Republic of China came into effect (January 1, 2008), the results may include some biases from the current staff conditions in either city. However, even with the rapidly changing wage levels in China, the survey findings can shed light on some of the production activities of staff in the Shanghai region.

4.4.1 Attributes of Staff Members

4.4.1.1 Basic Attributes

Animation production studio staff are generally employed under a contract system with contract periods from 1 to 3 years. At each expiry date, staff either renew their contracts or find new employment.[21] Forty-four of the 58 Shanghai production studio staff and 38 of the 53 Wuxi production studio staff worked on a contract basis. Shanghai production studio staff included eight freelancers and six with other or unknown status. However, Wuxi production studio staff included 12 freelancers and three with other or unknown status. According to Yamashita (2008), the employment contract system was introduced to eliminate the "iron rice bowl (tie fan wan)"[22] of the permanent employment system, and it is common to establish the expiry of employment contracts.[23] It is thought that the contract basis predominates in the employment system in China because of such labor relationships.

Most Shanghai production studio staff are paid based on their completed output (31 staff), and other staff received commission payment (12 staff), fixed salaries (10 staff), and other or unknown basis (five staff). A similar case was observed at Wuxi production studios, 41 staff were paid based on their completed output and 10 staff received commission payment. However, only two staff received fixed salaries. In both cities, many payments are based on completed output and commission and therefore are unstable.

In 2007, the average annual income of general workers in Shanghai and Wuxi was 34,707 yuan (2,892 yuan/month)[24] and 34,375 yuan (2,865 yuan/month),[25] respectively. In comparison, the average monthly income of Shanghai production studio staff was 4,172 yuan, with 18 out of the 58 staff earning 2,500 yuan or more and less than 5,000 yuan per month. The average monthly income of Wuxi production studio staff was 3,148 yuan, with the majority of staff (33 out of 52) earning 2,500 yuan or more and less than 5,000 yuan/month.

---

[21] The Labor Contract Law of the People's Republic of China (hereafter new law), effective January 1, 2008, requires permanent employment upon continuous service of 10 years or more, or third contract renewal (Article 14, Paragraph 3.1.3). As the questionnaire survey took place before the new law came into effect, there were no such employment constraints. Furthermore, a similar survey was attempted in June 2008, but the response was rejected on the grounds of the new law enforced. These circumstances suggest that production studios are undecided about what their employment contracts should be.

[22] The iron rice bowl (tie fan wan) refers to employment security funded by the government.

[23] The employment contract system was enacted as described in Chapter 3, "Labor contract," the Labor Law of the People's Republic of China (old law) as legislated in 1994. Subsequently, the law was amended in connection with a new legislation issued in June 2007, which became effective as of January 1, 2008.

[24] Xinmin Evening News (2008): http://www.news365.com.cn/wxpd/zc/jyzd/200803/t20080325_1807336.htm (last accessed on July 13, 2014).

[25] National Bureau of Statistics of China (2008): http://www.stats.gov.cn/ztjc/ztfx/dfxx/200804/t20080416_34108.html (last accessed on July 13, 2014).

Table 4.5 Distribution of employees' monthly income and years of employment

Years of employment	Monthly income (Unit: 10,000 yuan)					
	<2,500	<5,000	<7,500	7,500≤	Unknown	Total
<2		2/–	2/–	1/–	1/–	6/–
2	6/2	4/6	2/–	1/–	1/–	14/8
3	3/3	2/3				6/6
4	–/5	1/2				1/7
5	–/2	5/8	2/–	–/1		7/11
6	1/–	2/5	2/–	2/–	–/1	7/6
7	1/–	–/3	–/1	1/–		2/4
8			1/1	2/–		3/1
9	–/1		–/1	1/–		1/2
10		2/2		2/–		4/2
11						
12		–/2				–/2
13			2/–		1/–	3/–
14	–/1	–/2	1/–			1/3
15≤	–/1		1/–	1/–	1/–	3/1
Total	11/15	18/33	13/3	12/1	4/1	58/53

Source: Questionnaire survey
Note: The figure indicates the number of staff in each category at Shanghai and Wuxi studios

Table 4.5 presents the monthly income according to the number of years worked. According to this table, income for Shanghai production studio staff tends to increase with the number of years worked. In contrast, the income of many Wuxi production studio staff remained below 5,000 yuan regardless of the number of years worked. At the same time, many staff earned more than the monthly income of the average general worker in both cities.

Shanghai production studio staff included those who performed creative department work, such as "producer" (three staff), "supervisor" (four staff), in addition to those who performed production department work such as "animation picture" (22 staff), "key picture" (12 staff), and "coloring" (five staff) (Table 4.6). Furthermore, four of the 10 staff performing other tasks also performed creative department work. These data suggest that Shanghai production studio staff offered technical skills across a wide range of production processes. In contrast, among Wuxi production studio staff, one staff member performs "producer" work while four perform "director," which falls under the management department. Furthermore, while 10 staff also perform additional tasks, one performs creative department work. Many staff are exclusively involved in specific production department work such as "animation picture" (32 staff), "coloring" (seven staff). The number of Wuxi production studio staff involved in creative department work is small compared with Shanghai production studio staff.

Some Shanghai production studios conduct business with production studios in multiple countries or produce their own products for the domestic market.

Table 4.6 Number of surveyed workers by job fields

Job fields	Shanghai	Wuxi
Producer	3 (3)	1 (1)
Director	5 (3)	4 (1)
Supervisor	4 (2)	0
Key picture	12 (1)	2 (2)
Animation picture	22 (3)	41 (9)
Coloring	5 (3)	11 (4)
Background	1 (0)	3 (3)
Shooter	0	0
Sound	3 (1)	0
Editor	0	0
3D/CG	10 (1)	0
Other	3 (0)	1 (0)
Respondents	58	53

Source: Questionnaire survey
Note: Numbers in parentheses represent workers with multiple job fields

Furthermore, business ties were established with other studios in the same industry to supplement labor and skills. Shanghai studios find the abundant supply of labor involved in creative department work in addition to production department work appealing, although such labor is costly compared with that in the provinces. In contrast, the business of the Wuxi production studios specializes in the production department where they receive orders from Japanese production studios. The fact that many Wuxi production studio staff members work in the production department reflects the business scope of the studios where they work.

4.4.1.2   Forms of Labor Supply

According to Studio H, few vocational training schools specialize in animation production in China. While a major subject at universities such as Beijing Film Academy exists, few graduate with a major in this subject. In addition, those graduates are technically immature and acquire their skills during employment. Considering final educational background, junior college graduates (27 staff) form the largest group among Shanghai production studio staff. Twelve Shanghai production studio staff held bachelor's degrees (20.7 %), six of whom majored in courses related to animation. However, the largest group among Wuxi production studio staff is high school graduates (22 staff), followed by junior high or vocational high school[26] graduates (14 staff). There are only eight junior colleges and only four teach bachelor's degrees (7.5 %). Furthermore, only one staff member

---

[26] Vocational high schools represent one option following junior high school.

with a bachelor's degree had majored in a course related to animation. Shanghai production studios had more staff with higher education compared with Wuxi production studios. However, according to Studio H, many of its staff attended a technical school (no longer in existence) established by Studio α. While technical schools may function as potential training schools for labor, their impact was not captured in this survey.

Considering work experience, 27 Shanghai production studio staff (45.7 %) had worked in other industries, but only 33 (62.2 %) Wuxi production studio staff had worked elsewhere. Shanghai production studio staff had worked in the related content industry: film production (six staff), publishing (two staff), and game software development (one staff member). Seven staff worked in other industries. Work experience in the related content industry is likewise observed among Wuxi production studio staff, namely in advertising (eight staff), design (four staff), and data processing (three staff). However, compared with Shanghai staff, moves from the business services area are noticeable. Furthermore, there are many respondents in the "other" category, which suggests skills transfers from diverse industries.

Considering the reasons why staff chose the animation industry, popular responses for Shanghai studio staff were "I can utilize my skills" (26 staff), "I have always liked animation" (26 staff), "the industry has good prospects of development" (19 staff), and "there are few time constraints" (14 staff).[27] These responses reveal that in addition to the appeal of the industry and form of employment, staff chose work that involved creative activities or matched their preferences, such as being fond of watching animation and possessing good drawing skills.

However, similarly, popular responses among Wuxi production studio staff include "I can utilize my skills" (27 staff) and "the industry has good prospects of development" (22 staff). Many staff also responded "it pays well" (28 staff) and "work was easy to find" (20 staff).[28] Our interviews found that local employers recruit on an ongoing basis to secure their labor supply. It seems that this effort has resulted in the ease of finding work among available staff. Wuxi production studio staff attached relatively great importance to high level of income and large number of employment opportunities as determinants for taking up employment.

Studios were asked for their focus when hiring staff (Table 4.7). With the exception of studios G and I, which did not respond, all Shanghai production studios cited issues related to technical skills. Other responses included "work experience in the industry" (A, B, F) and "headhunting competent staff members away from other studios" (H). Responses from foreign-subcontracting- and foreign-funded-type studios included "diligence" (B), "endurance and enthusiasm" (C), and "personality" (D, F). It seems that particularly studios established to perform production department work

---

[27] Other responses provided by Shanghai production studio staff members were "no specific reason" (eight staff), "it pays well" (seven staff), "work was easy to find" (five staff), "other" (five staff), and "the work is stable" (two staff).

[28] Other responses provided by Wuxi production studio staff were "I have always liked animation" (14 staff), "there are few time constraints" (nine staff), "no specific reason" (eight staff), "the work is stable" (four staff), and "other" (one staff member).

Table 4.7   Important criteria for hiring workers at participating studios

Cities	Studios	Criteria
Shanghai	A	Work experience in the industry/technical skills
	B	Technical skills/diligence/work experience in the industry
	C	Technical skills/endurance and enthusiasm evaluated during trial period
		*Not much weight placed on communication skills
	D	Technical skills/personality evaluated during trial period
	E	Work experience in the industry/technical skills/cooperativeness
		*Basically only hire workers with experiences. New graduates with enthusiasm and interest, which guarantee they are hardworking, are hired rarely.
	F	Work experience in the industry/personality evaluated during trial period
		New graduates having no technological application are not preferred.
	G	–
	H	Technical skills/headhunting competent staff members away from other studios
		*New graduates have no immediate skills
	I	–
	J	Technical skills/diligence
Wuxi	K	Technical skills/personality
	L	–
	M	Technical skills

Source: Interview survey
Note: "–" indicates data not provided

with an international division of labor sought staff who can endure labor-intensive production activities. Studios K and M, the Wuxi production studios that responded, both cited "technical skills." Studio K also responded "personality." These studios are required to produce against tight deadlines set by Japanese production studios. Moreover, Wuxi production studio staff perform tasks in which they tend to specialize in labor-intensive processes such as animation picture and coloring. Consequently, studios K and M seek technical skills to fulfill large production volumes against tight deadlines while maintaining a consistent level of quality.

4.4.2   Actual State of Staff Relationships

4.4.2.1   Opportunities for Staff Members to Acquire Technical Skills

Concerning opportunities for staff to acquire technical skills (Table 4.8), the most popular response among Shanghai production studio staff was "guidance on the job from senior staff members" (24 staff), followed by "acquiring skills through self-education after joining the industry" (17 staff), "acquiring skills at educational

Table 4.8 Staff opportunities to acquire technical skills

Opportunities	Shanghai	Wuxi
Guidance on the job from senior staff members	24	21
Acquiring skills through self-education after joining the industry	17	4
Acquiring skills at educational establishments	12	6
Study groups comprising fellows	11	33
Training at previous studios	10	2
Training at current studio	7	1
Other	2	0
Unknown	2	0
Respondents	58	53

Source: Questionnaire survey
Multiple answers were permitted
Shanghai, Shanghai production studio staff; Wuxi, Wuxi production studio staff

establishments" (12 staff), and "study groups comprising fellows" (11 staff). Other responses included "training at previous studios" (ten staff) and "training at current studio" (seven staff). A fair number of Shanghai production studio staff acquired technical skills through relationships with fellows ("guidance on the job from senior staff members," "study groups comprising fellows"). However, the most popular response from Wuxi production studio staff was "study groups comprising fellows" (33 staff), followed by "guidance on the job from senior staff members" (21 staff). Wuxi production studio staff indicated that they acquired technical skills through their relationships with other staff. These findings show that relationships with other staff played an important role in the acquisition of technical skills.

4.4.2.2   Opportunities for Staff to Obtain Work

As indicated in previous chapters, staff members obtained work using personal connections in the animation industry. Staff members avoided income instability through involvement in multiple productions. To examine whether a similar trend could be observed in China, staff were asked about their friends and acquaintances who helped them to obtain work and the number of jobs in which they were involved during a 1-month period. The results reveal that many respondents obtained multiple jobs through their connections with other staff members. Twenty-three of the 50 Shanghai production studio staff had work referral contacts. In particular, more than the half of staff members with unstable forms of pay such as payment on completed output or commission pay have one or more work referral contacts. However, 49 of 51 Wuxi production studio staff had one or more work referral contacts.

On jobs contracted during a 1-month period, 38 of the 50 Shanghai respondents work full-time at the studio where they are employed. Twelve respondents work on productions of multiple products at multiple studios. The occupation types of the 12 respondents range across the overall production processes: "director" (one staff member), "supervisor" (one staff member), "key picture" (four staff), "sound" (two staff), "computer graphic" (one staff member), "other" (one staff member), both creative and directing department work (one staff member), and both creative and production department work (one staff member). Among Shanghai production studio staff, no differences were observed depending on the types of tasks of staff who used work referral contacts. However, as for Wuxi production studio staff, 42 of the 49 respondents worked full-time at the studio where they are employed. Furthermore, three out of the four staff members in "director" were involved in a large number of productions compared with the average among Wuxi production studio staff (four productions ordered from 1.6 studios per month). The number of jobs they contracted was 10 productions at 10 studios, 15 productions at 6 studios, and 12 productions at 6 studios, respectively. "Director" staff act as contacts for Japanese production studios and perform management tasks such as the local allocation of labor (Fig. 4.8). The large quantity of work they take on reflects the volume of work from Japanese production studios. It also suggests that they act as work referral contacts in Wuxi.

4.4.3 Reasons for Continuing to Work in Cities

Why do staff continue to work in Shanghai or Wuxi? Many Shanghai production studio staff responded that they continue to work there because of "large number of production studios" (24 staff) and "the attraction of Shanghai" (22 staff) (Table 4.9). Responses also included "the large number of colleagues" (17 staff), "presence of person I want to work with" (13 staff), and "ease of obtaining inside industry information" (13 staff). They valued the proximity to production studios and other staff members and felt that Shanghai held sufficient attraction for them to continue working in the city.[29] However, the most popular response from Wuxi production studio staff was "large number of production studios" (42 staff), followed by "the large number of colleagues" (23 staff), "presence of person I want to work with" (21 staff), and "ease of obtaining inside industry information" (19 staff). Similarly to Shanghai production studio staff, they valued connections with other staff. However, while many cited "ease of enjoying services on the job"[30] (18 staff), very few responded with "the attraction of Wuxi" (four staff) as opposed to the small number of respondents among Shanghai production studio staff. In other words, a large number of responses seeking actual benefit for employment can be observed.

---

[29] Clear responses cannot be received in relation to the essence of the attraction. However, respondents may have referred to the modern atmosphere of the metropolis, judging from the responses provided by spin-off-type studios for their choice of city location such as "rich qualified worker with high levels of cultural appreciation" (G) and it being "the birthplace of the animation industry" (J, H).

[30] Services on the job refer to the necessary in-house facilities and infrastructure of the surrounding areas for executing work.

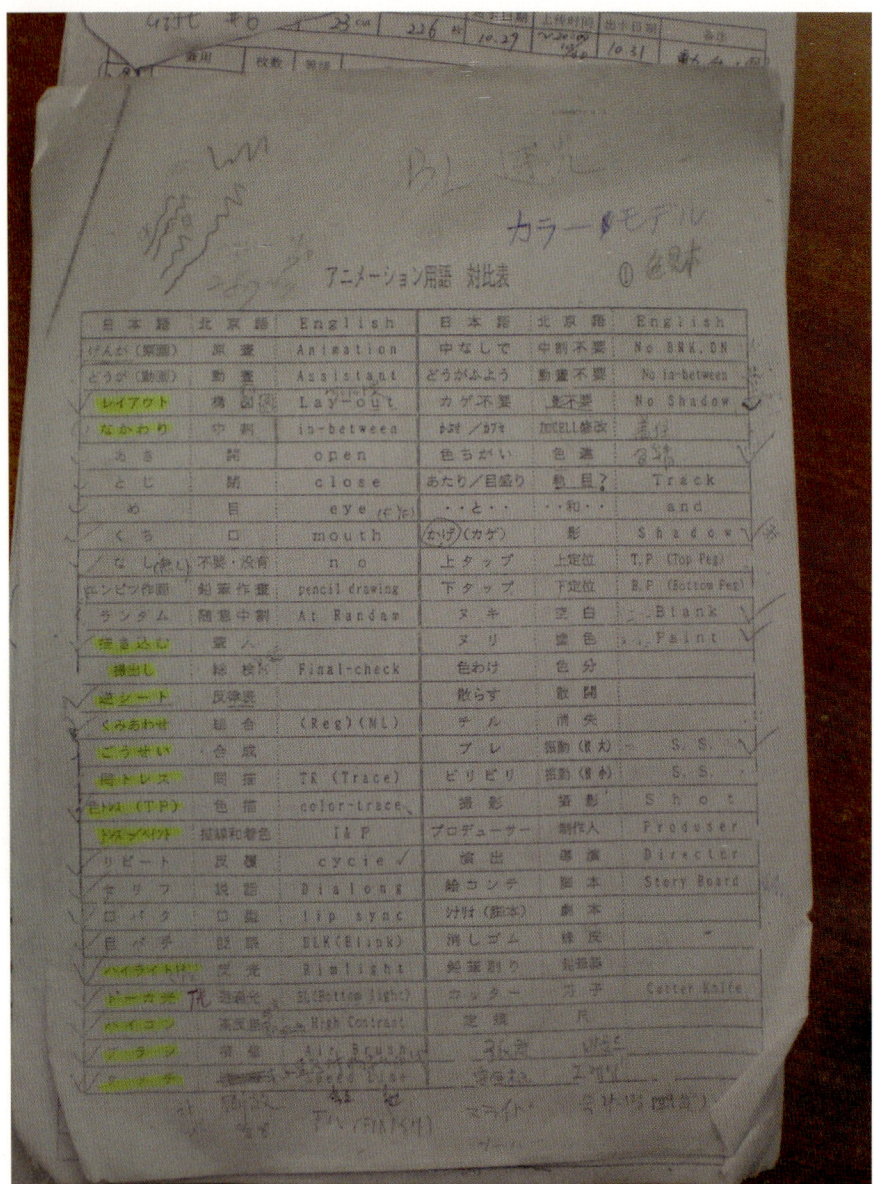

Fig. 4.8 Parallel translation list of animation terms in a studio in Wuxi. *Note*: The instructions from Japanese studios are written in Japanese. The leaders check the instructions with parallel translation lists and give directions to their staff

Table 4.9 Participating workers' reasons for continuing to work in Shanghai/Wuxi

Reasons	Shanghai	Wuxi
Large number of production studios	24	41
Attractiveness of Shanghai/Wuxi	22	4
Large number of colleagues	17	23
Presence of person I want to work with	13	21
Ease of obtaining inside industry information	13	19
Convenient transportation	9	3
Ease of enjoying services on the job	4	18
Many side jobs	3	1
Others	7	0
Respondents	58	53

Source: Questionnaire survey
Multiple answers were permitted

4.5 Conclusion

In concluding this chapter, we present the agglomeration structure of this industry in the Shanghai region by combining the findings obtained through the cases studies in Chaps. 2 and 3 (Fig. 4.9).

The Chinese animation industry has demonstrated remarkable growth in recent years, and the potential size of the domestic market is huge. However, the domestic market is still emerging. The production activities of the industry mainly involve subcontracting from foreign production studios such as those in Japan and the United States. The Chinese government and local government are putting regulations such as broadcast restrictions for overseas products and support policies into effect to foster the domestic market. With these developments, the Shanghai region is becoming a locus of agglomeration of the animation industry within China.

Reviewing the reasons for the choice of location, studios with close ties with foreign production studios at their inception and in subsequent stages of development cite the abundant supply of labor needed for the labor-intensive production processes involved. They also emphasize the importance of access to the international airport, which is used for international business. Accessibility of the international airport was also recognized as an issue for the Seoul animation industry and is an important factor in the choice of location for production studios that rely on business with foreign companies for their operations. In contrast, the abundant supply of labor was not identified in the Seoul case study. Seoul production studios consider their staff members' technical skills and creativity. Recently, orders from foreign production studios received by South Korean animation production studios have been shifting from production department to creative department work. In contrast, labor-intensive production activities are sought from Chinese production studios, which take on production department work. This difference in roles within the international division of labor is emerging as a qualitative difference in the type of labor sought by each location. Furthermore, some Wuxi production studios cite the tacit

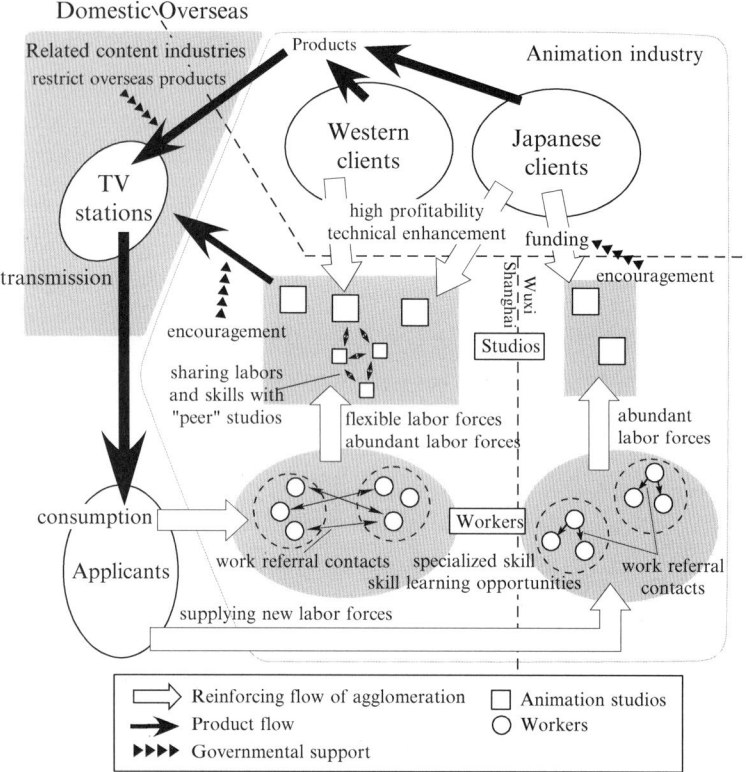

Fig. 4.9 Agglomeration structure model of animation industry in the Shanghai region

approval of late-night labor and expectations of preferential treatment policies as reasons for choosing their location. Government measures for preferential treatment were not encountered in the case studies on Tokyo and Seoul. This governmental impact is specific to the Shanghai region.

With a focus on the relatively large Shanghai production studios, some studios are expanding in the domestic market by using the related content industry for their clients. These studios locate themselves in Shanghai to gain proximity to their clients in the related content industry. Proximity to the related content industry was also identified in Tokyo and Seoul and is an essential factor in the choice of location of animation studios producing products for the domestic market.

In Tokyo and Seoul, one of the factors stimulating the agglomeration of studios is the existence of quick delivery and complementary business relations with peer studios located in the vicinity. An inspection of business relationships with other studios in the same industry in the Shanghai region reveals that Shanghai studios have business relationships with peer studios such as studios they were affiliated with prior to their spin-off and those established by former colleagues. This tendency can be observed particularly between the small studios. In these instances, relationships are established so that studios can complement skills and labor in order to meet tight deadlines. In addition, a relationship of mutual trust among those studios is built in order to hedge against business risk. In this way, production studios locate themselves in Shanghai to establish ongoing business ties with other studios in the same industry.

The payment system shows high incidences of commission pay and payment based on completed output, which indicates income instability. In Shanghai, reasons for staff to choose employment in this industry include their future prospects in the industry and the appealing form of employment, in addition to their employment matching their preferences and allowing them to enjoy creative activities. In Wuxi, the reasons include expectations of a high income and the easiness of finding work. Many staff members acquire technical skills during employment through relationships with other staff members, such as study groups comprising fellows and guidance from senior staff. Additionally, while staff essentially work full-time at the studio where they are employed, some obtain multiple jobs through referrals by friends and acquaintances' work referral contacts. Staff stay on to work in Shanghai and Wuxi because they seek proximity to studios and collegial relationships. The flexible and skilled labor force developed in abundance through staff relationships is indispensable to studios providing labor-intensive production within the international division of labor to exploit the domestic market through sales of their own products and maintain stable operations through business to supplement skills.

The structure of reproducing labor through staff relationships was also identified in the cases of Tokyo and Seoul. The abundant, flexible, and skilled workforce in metropolitan regions is itself emerging as a factor that reinforces the metropolitan agglomeration of animation production studios.

References

Development Research Center of the State Administration of Radio Film and Television (2006) 2006 nian Zhongguo Guangbo Dianying Dianshi Fazhan Baogao [Report on development of China's radio, film and television 2006]. Social Sciences Academic Press, Beijing

Editorial Board of China Animation Yearbook (ed) (2006) Zhongguo Donghua Nianjian 2006 [Yearbook of Chinese animation 2006]. China Radio and TV Press, Beijing

Lu H (2011) 2010 nian Zhongguo Donghua Dianshipian Fazhan Baogao [Report on development of China's animated television series in 2010]. In: Lu B, Zheng Y, Niu X (eds) Zhongguo Dongman Chanye Fazhan Baogao [Report on China animation industry]. Social Sciences Academic Press, Beijing (Chinese)

Qin X (2006) Zhongguo Donghuapian de Chanye Jingjixue Yanjiu [The economics of China's animation industry]. China Market Press, Beijing

Yamamoto K (2012) Animeshon Sangyo no Bungyo Kankei to Chiiki Seisaku [Division of labor relationships and local policies]. In: Tsunatoshi I, Masaya Y (eds) Sangyo Shuseki no Henbo to Chiiki Seisaku: Gurokaru Jidai no Chiiki Sangyo Kenkyu [The changes of industrial agglomeration and local polices – studies for local industries in the glocal era]. Minerva Shobo, Kyoto, pp 195–215 (Japanese)

Yamashita N (2008) Chugoku Rodo Keiyaku Ho no Naiyo to Sono Igi [The contents of the Chinese Labor Contract Law and its significance]. Jpn J Labour Stud 576:35–44

Zhang S (2006) Huigu Zhongguo Donghua 80 nian Fazhan Lecheng [Recalling the 80-year course of development of the Chinese animation]. Editorial Board of China Animation Yearbook (ed) Zhongguo donghua nianjian 2006 [Yearbook of Chinese animation 2006]. China Radio and TV Press, Beijing

Chapter 5
Animation Workers and the Studio as a Creative Nexus in Tokyo: Studio M Workers' Daily Activities

Abstract This chapter explores the spatial functions of animation studios by focusing on workers' use of space as seen in a case study of an animation studio in Tokyo. This analysis uses a time-geographical method to document studio workers' daily activities. Workers' behavior differs depending on their job type. Production department workers tend to stay in their jobs at the studio for a long time, acquiring skills with advice from senior workers while on the job and building social networks through conversation while waiting for jobs to start. Directing department workers schedule projects, and they transport half-finished products to and from other studios and frequently confer with workers in- and outside their own studio. Animation studios offer their workers not only various forms of infrastructure, but also opportunities for face-to-face communication, which is indispensable in producing animation. The studios, therefore, are "creative nexuses."

Keywords Creators • Directors • Personal networks • Tokyo • Working environment

5.1 Introduction

5.1.1 Context

We have explored the structure of agglomeration in the animation industry under the influences of domestic markets and the international division of labor among East Asian countries with a focus on the characteristics of labor markets and transactional relationships between studios. However, before this study is concluded, the function of studios and the characteristics of workers' creative activities should be discussed.

This chapter focuses on studio worker behavior and their intramural environments, and is intended to promote a more detailed discussion of industrial agglomeration. A discussion of these matters is essential to understanding the structure of agglomeration because workers can influence their studios just as studios influence their workers' creativity; hence, workers can also influence the agglomeration process.

© Springer Japan 2014

K. Yamamoto, *The Agglomeration of the Animation Industry in East Asia*,
International Perspectives in Geography: AJG Library 4,
DOI 10.1007/978-4-431-55093-8_5

Even in a world filled with modern information technologies, face-to-face communication is an important part of creative productivity (Stoper and Venables 2004). Thus, metropolises consisting of several types of industrial clusters are important for development within the content industry. However, some studies argue that the lifestyle and working conditions of end workers are also important factors in attracting these types of industries to a metropolis. For example, Arai et al. (2004) reveal both the spatial characteristics and the clusters of multimedia and Internet businesses in central Tokyo utilizing both geographical information systems techniques and questionnaires administered to firms and laborers in those industries. In their article, they point out that the Shibuya neighborhood of Tokyo has grown rapidly to become a new center of multimedia and Internet content business. The one factor that they suggest has been responsible for this development is the difference in the favored residential environments of technical workers and creative workers[1]: technical workers prefer to live in the suburbs, whereas creative laborers prefer intersuburban areas. Their theory suggests that the creative workers' proximity to Shibuya has enticed multimedia and Internet content businesses to locate nearby so that they can employ these creative laborers. Many of the researchers cited in Chap. 1 have indicated the importance of human networks for creative production (e.g., Vinodrai 2006; Blair 2003; Bain 2004, 2005; Hara 2005).

Many of these studies also attempted to examine the effect of social relationships and the workplace on productivity and creative output. Although workers are expected to mutually interact with their workspaces, it is still debatable whether and how the creative activities of workers affect their workspaces. Accordingly, I have studied the daily activities of creative people producing creative products at an animation studio. The findings will help to clarify our actual image of an animation studio's workspace. Previous studies on this topic have not focused on how the creative products are made. In other words, they do not explain how workers generate creative output in their workspaces. By describing studio workers' activities, this study will reveal the functions a studio serves, with a particular focus on how workers build relationships with their colleagues and how they produce creative materials. These details of the process used to facilitate worker creativity have not been adequately described in previous studies.

5.1.2   Japanese Animation Production Process and Worker Careers

Japanese animated films consist of several drawn pictures per frame. Figure 5.1 shows the production schedule of a 25-minute episode in a TV animation series at the point when Studio M has received the work after the layout process. As already mentioned in Chap. 2, it is common for lower processes to be compressed to make

---

[1]According to Arai et al. (2004), "technical workers" engage in the fields of software/systems design, software/systems maintenance, and programming. On the other hand, "creative workers" are involved in designing the Web, audio materials, graphics, and publishing materials.

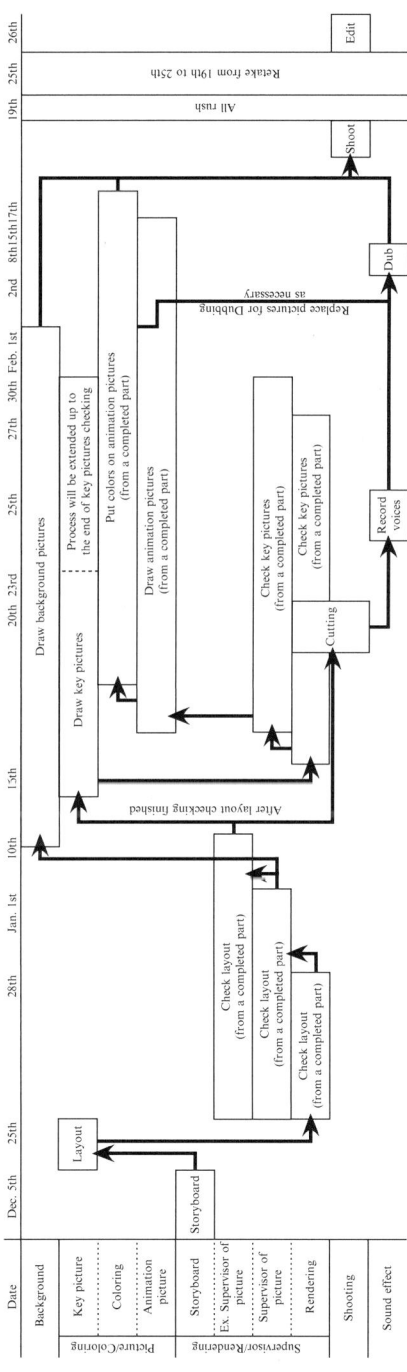

Fig. 5.1 Production schedule of a 25-minute episode of an animated TV series. *Source*: Interviews survey

up for delays in the upper processes. In this case, however, the work had not been completed more than 1 month after the original deadline because of delays in the upper processes, such as the checking process by the Rendering and supervisor.

In all, about 150 people are required to produce a single episode of an animated TV series, but the total number of workers associated with the series cannot be counted by simply multiplying the number of episodes by 150.[2]

In the Japanese animation industry, workers acquire skills and techniques through their daily jobs and eventually obtain more advanced jobs that require more sophisticated skills (see Chap. 2). In the United States, the skill sets of animation workers can be guaranteed by The Animation Guild, IATSE Local 839, and they can improve their careers by passing a certification exam. In Japan, on the other hand, no such labor associations or career-advancement systems exist, and the techniques of animation workers are assessed on the basis of the history of the animated productions in which they have taken part or the studio to which they belong. According to our interviews with several types of workers in the animation industry, workers' career paths are generally divided into two types with different technical requirements. One path is that of a supervisor or character designer. On this path, workers start their careers in the animation picture department. Those with superior skills can become supervisors or character designers after acquiring experience in the animation picture, key picture, and storyboard departments. The other path is that of a director. Those who are employed in the directing department and have learned how to manage whole projects can become producers (Fig. 5.2).

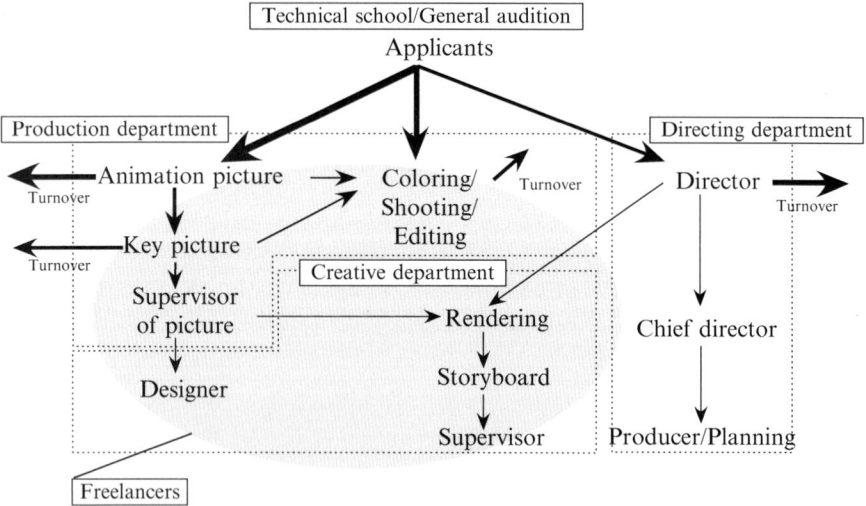

Fig. 5.2 Major career paths of animation workers in Japan. *Source*: Interview survey

---

[2] Workers may be associated with several projects in a single year, and their jobs are not seasonal as they are in Los Angeles (Scott 1988). The directing department manages the production schedule and transports half-finished drawings to the departments in charge of other processes. Directors handle several projects at the same time (Table 5.4).

5.1.3 Methodology

The main methodology for this portion of the study used a questionnaire survey and interviews to assess studio workers' daily activities. In addition to these, a full day of observation was performed while shadowing one of the participating directors at an animation studio (Studio M). At Studio M, five staff members from the animation picture department and five from the directing department participated in the survey. These two departments were the subjects of the investigation because they are involved in the end process of the industry. The workers in these departments produce creative materials by hand every day and are on the leading edge of creativity in animation production. Furthermore, the animation picture and directing departments are entry points for workers starting out in the industry. In other words, these workers are some of the actors who constitute the "core" described by Throsby (2001, p. 113). The survey of workers' daily activities traces the processes involved in producing creative materials and obtaining new techniques.

Studio M was established in 1986 with an initial investment of ten million yen[3] and is located in Suginami Ward, Tokyo. The studio consists of 34 staff members and is divided into five departments: administrative (three staff members), directing (nine staff members), key/animation picture (12 staff members), coloring (eight staff members), and editing (four staff members). It takes orders for partial episodes, whole episodes, or whole series. The basic characteristics of the staff, such as their payment systems, average working times, and monthly salaries, are in agreement with those reported for animation workers in general as reported by the Japan Institute for Labor Policy and Training (2005) and in Chap. 2 of this book. Thus, both Studio M and its staff are considered typical of the industry and are appropriate subjects for our research.

The questionnaire consists of two parts. The first part contains multiple-choice questions that establish the basic characteristics of the respondents, while the second part is an open questionnaire using a time-geographical method to record the interviewees' daily activities. The first half of the questionnaire is based on the one used in the my previous study and was distributed to animation studio staff in Japan, South Korea, and China (see Chaps. 2, 3, and 4). The questionnaire entries detail the respondent's age, income, reason for working in the animation industry, and so on. The latter part is an activity diary covering a period of 72 h, from 12:00 a.m. on December 15 to 12:00 a.m. on December 18, 2009. This method refers to the study by Arai et al. (1996). The activity diary includes behaviors and a transportation questionnaire.[4] The record of vehicle logs at Studio M enhances the reliability of the data. One of the directors participating in the investigation was shadowed for 12 h to observe the details of the director's activities, communication, and travel, such as

---

[3] 100 yen = 0.87 US dollars as of December 1, 2009.

[4] Respondents may feel burdened by the requirement of recording the same behaviors several times in a day, and it is expected that staff members may record responses that are at variance with the facts. However, the record could be extracted by comparing the data, as with Arai et al. (1996).

the time the director spent on each activity and the destinations and purposes of the director's trips. In addition to the general survey, a supplementary e-mail and telephone survey of two workers, one director and one animation picture member, was conducted in March and June 2010, and a supplementary interview with an administrative member was conducted in June 2011.

In studies on the animation industry, previous researchers have seldom focused on the daily activities of individual staff members. One of the reasons for this is because it can be difficult to convince staff members to participate because this type of research is time-consuming. I had cultivated personal exchanges with Studio M for more than 2 years before requesting cooperation for the research, and had the opportunity to implement the research and obtain detailed data from ten staff members. This level of detail ensures that the survey is truly suggestive of the daily production activity of workers in this creative industry and the actual conditions in the spaces where they work.

5.2   Survey and Analysis

5.2.1   Studio M Working Environment

Table 5.1 shows the basic characteristics of interviewees. In most cases, the studio's departments use different payment systems: with the exception of C1, workers in the animation picture department were paid based on their completed output, and the salaries of three of the five interviewees in the animation picture department were under 100,000 yen per month. C1, on the other hand, earned a fixed salary of 150,000 yen, which can be regarded as a stable income by workers in the different

Table 5.1 Basic characteristics of interviewees

ID	Age (sex)	Former job	Length of service	Hometown	Average daily working hours	Wage system	Monthly income
C1	29 (F)	–	7	Nagano	8	Fixed	150
C2	29 (F)	Welfare	1	Tokyo	9	Piecework	110
C3	23 (F)	–	1	Tokyo	14	Piecework	70
C4	22 (M)	–	1	Saitama	10	Piecework	50
C5	20 (M)	–	1	Kanagawa	9	Piecework	30
D1	26 (M)	–	6	Hyogo	13	Fixed	190
D2	28 (M)	–	5	Chiba	14	Fixed	190
D3	29 (M)	Service	3	Kagawa	10	Fixed	200
D4	23 (M)	–	3	Tokyo	12	Fixed	190
D5	32 (M)	Multimedia	1	Chiba	15	Fixed	180

Source: Questionnaire survey
Notes: Length of service in given in years. Monthly income is given in 1000 yen. "C" in ID indicates that the worker is a "creator," such as an animation picture worker, while "D" indicates that the worker is in the directing department

departments. C2 also earns more than 100,000 yen per month, but between 25 and 50 % of C2's salary comes from secondary business; C2's monthly salary earned by actually drawing pictures is less than 100,000 yen.[5] In contrast, workers in the directing department receive fixed salaries between 180,000 and 200,000 yen— even the low end of this range is higher than C1's salary, the highest salary in the animation picture department. According to the National Tax Agency (2010), Studio M staff receive lower-than-average salaries for workers in a company with a capital of less than 20 million yen. According to the statistics, male and female workers in Japan in their early 20s receive, on average, 186,000 and 163,000 yen, respectively, while those in their late 20s receive 266,000 and 204,000 yen, respectively.

The departmental differences in payment systems are attributed to the differences in the characteristics of the departments. It is reasonable to evaluate the animation picture staff according to the quantity and quality of their drawings because ability and technique differ between one staff member and the next. In contrast, it is harder to quantify the work of directors because their main job is to schedule project adjustments and negotiate with subcontractors.

Interviewees in the animation picture departments had all been employed for 1 year, except for C1, who had been working at Studio M for 7 years.[6] There was greater variety in the duration of employment for workers in the directing department: one worker had 1 year of experience at Studio M, two had 3 years, one had 5 years, and one had 6 years.

The academic backgrounds of the interviewees were high school (C2 and C5), technical school (C1, C4, D1, D4, and D5), or university (C3, D2, and D3). Two staff members in the animation picture department and three in the directing department had attended technical school. It is important to note that half of those workers who had never worked in an industry other than the animation industry had attended technical school.[7]

Workers who transitioned directly from high school or a 4-year college degree into the animation industry (C2, C3, C5, D2, D3, and D5) had varying reasons for choosing to work in the animation industry, but the primary reason for most was that they liked animation. Some animation picture staff reported that animation picture drawing was a less time-consuming job or that it was easy to obtain a job in the field. They also listed some other attractive factors. For example, C2 was interested in animation production and C3 liked to watch and draw animation and had a desire to become an artist. While the reasons given by animation picture workers are favorable to the animation industry, directors listed more passive or practical reasons.

---

[5] C2 is the only interviewee who mentioned a secondary job.

[6] The animation picture department of Studio M has ten staff members: three whose employment durations were more than 5 years, three who have been employed for 2–4 years, and four who have been employed less than a year. However, there were no interviewees from staff who had been employed for 2 to 4 years, and there was only one interviewee who had been employed for more than 5 years. Thus, this study is not representative in this respect.

[7] The former jobs of these midcareer interviewees are in multimedia-related services (D5), service (D3), and welfare (C2) industries.

D3 obtained a job in the animation industry in order to move to Tokyo, and D5 wanted to use the skills acquired in D5's former job. D2 listed passive reasons including that it was easy to obtain jobs in the animation industry and that there were no other job offerings.

The average daily working time of interviewees in the animation picture department is 8–14 h. This is longer than the average working time at weekday of workers in Japan, which is 7.09 h (Statistics Bureau, Ministry of Internal Affairs and Communications 2012). The average daily working time of interviewees in the directing department is 10 h minimum, which is longer than the average working time in the animation picture department. Although directors earn a fixed payment and a higher salary than animation picture workers, they work longer hours and their wage rates are still comparatively low. These data indicate that low wages and long working times are common working conditions in the industry.

With C1's 7 years at Studio M, C1 is the most noteworthy interviewee in this study. C1 is the oldest person in the animation picture department and is the only worker in the department who receives a fixed salary. C1's skills as an animation picture worker are highly valued, and C1 has had opportunities to advance to higher-level jobs, such as "layout" or "key picture." However, C1 has requested to continue working as an animation picture drawer, and Studio M, aware of the benefit of C1's mentorship of younger drawers, granted C1's request and has allowed C1 to stay in the animation picture department. It is hard to quantify the value of C1's teaching ability in a piecework context, but C1's skills are nonetheless highly valued by Studio M. Accordingly, Studio M has guaranteed a stable income for C1, which encourages C1 to stay at the studio.

5.2.2 Staff Residential Environment

All of the animation picture staff live with their parents except for C1, who lives with a partner. In the directing department, only D5 lives with a partner; the other directors live alone. All of the animation picture staff except C1 could not live alone because their unstable payment system and low salaries require them to receive monetary support from their parents. Those who receive a fixed salary of more than 150,000 yen, including C1 and the directors, can barely afford to live alone or with a partner.

Table 5.2 shows that staff commute time is dependent on their income. For example, animation picture staff, except C1, spend more than 1 h commuting, but C1 and four of the five directors live within a 30-minute commute.

Knowledge of Tokyo's spatial structure is important for understanding what household composition and commuting time reveal about staff members. The business district of Tokyo is concentrated on the eastern side of the city and most people live on the western side or in neighboring regions such as Saitama Prefecture north of Tokyo, Kanagawa Prefecture southwest of Tokyo, or Chiba Prefecture east of

Table 5.2 Residential districts and commuting circumstances

ID	Residential district	Transportation to the studio	Commuting time
C1	Suginami Ward, Tokyo	Walking	10
C2	Ota Ward, Tokyo	Bicycle	80
C3	Meguro Ward, Tokyo	Train	60
C4	Kasukabe City, Saitama	Train	120
C5	Sagamihara City, Kanagawa	Train	90
D1	Setagaya Ward, Tokyo	Train	25
D2	Suginami Ward, Tokyo	Motorbike	20
D3	Suginami Ward, Tokyo	Walking	30
D4	Suginami Ward, Tokyo	Walking	25
D5	Inagi City, Tokyo	Car or motorbike	50

Source: Daily activity survey and interview survey
Note: Commuting time is given in minutes

Tokyo.[8] As in other metropolises, many white-collar workers have gathered in dormitory suburbs where they own detached houses. Such office workers commute to urban Tokyo using an advanced network of public transportation. Kasukabe City, Saitama Prefecture, and Sagamihara City, Kanagawa Prefecture—the residential towns of C4 and C5, respectively—are typical satellite cities and dormitory suburbs of Tokyo. The average rent on a "one-room" apartment[9] located the same distance from Studio M as the nearest station to the studio is around 65,000 yen.[10] The staff household composition and commute time are defined by both the spatial structure of Tokyo and the payment system.

Participating workers who did not live with their parents, which include C1 and the directors, were asked about when they left their homes and why they chose the places where they live (Table 5.3). Four of them changed their residences when they were hired or within a year after being hired (D1, D3, D4, and D5).

C1 provides a unique example to demonstrate that income is the major determinant of a staff member's residential conditions. C1 was paid per completed job early in C1's career, and, not surprisingly, C1's salary was low. C1 lived with a younger sister, who was attending technical school, and needed support from C1's parents. Five years after C1 started with Studio M, when C1's father died and C1's sister returned home to look after their family, C1 started living with C1's partner, who worked as a director at Studio M and had previously lived alone. Another year later, C1 and C1's partner moved to a new home close to the studio because their previous

---

[8] Kanagawa, Saitama, Chiba, and Tokyo constitute the Minami–Kanto region. More than half of the interviewees, specifically, four animation picture staff members (Tokyo, 2; Kanagawa, 1; Saitama, 1), not including C1, and three directors (Tokyo, 1; Chiba, 2), not including D1 and D3, are from the region (see Table 5.1).

[9] A "one-room" apartment in Japan is similar to a studio apartment.

[10] The rental fee at market is based on results from the following estate agents' Web sites: "*Chintai HOME'S* (http://chintai.homes.co.jp/)" (retrieved June 15, 2010) and "*Mappion Sumai Sagashi* (http://realestate.mapion.co.jp/)" (retrieved June 15, 2010).

Table 5.3 Moves of interviewees and their residential preferences

| | | Cohabitants | | |
ID	Timing of recent move (years after employment)	Before move	After move	Reasons for choosing residence
C1	6 years ago	Sister	Partner	Partner was living there.
	5 years ago	Partner	Partner	Close to Studio M. Pet allowed.
D1	6 years ago (when employed)	–	–	Easy access to Studio M and urban areas.
D2	2.5 years ago	Family	–	Close to Studio M, Studio β and subcontractors
D3	1 year ago	Family	–	Close to Studio M, within walking distance.
D4	3 years ago (when employed)	Family	–	Close to Studio M, within walking distance.
D5	6 months ago	Family	Partner	Studio M owned the residence so the rent was low.
				Automobile commuting permitted.
				Close to the freelancers and easy to receive products from them.

Source: Interview survey
Note: Only interviewees without family cohabitants are included here

home was not big enough for two people and was an hour away from the studio. Eventually, the studio began to reward C1 for C1's skills and C1's salary increased to a level allowing C1 to support C1's partner, who was unemployed at the time of the interview.

D1's reason for moving was that D1 had obtained employment in Tokyo and needed to move there. D1 chose D1's new residence because of the convenience of transportation. D1's nearest station is on the same line as the station nearest to Studio M, which saves D1 the need to transfer when commuting. It is also easy for D1 to access central Tokyo because the nearest station to D1's residence offers access to that train line as well.

D3 moved to a place with a 30-minute walk to Studio M because D3's family home in Chiba was 90 min away from the studio by train, and the commuting time was causing D3 stress at work. D5 also listed commuting time as D5's motive for moving; D5 moved to a house owned by the studio located 50 min by car from the studio. D5 cited the cheap rent and convenient environment for D5's work as reasons for choosing that house. Several other animation workers live in D5's neighborhood, which makes it is easy for them to receive and transport half-finished products between the animation workers and the studios.[11]

In Japan, it is common for people to live with their parents even when they could sustain themselves on their own income, and independence from parents is not necessarily essential to being regarded as an adult. However, a correlation between staff

---

[11] The other reasons given were "Father has died and sister had to return home (C1's first move)," "took in a little kitten" (C1's second move), and "kicked out of my home" (D2).

members' income and independence from their parents was observed in this study, which also noted that working time efficiency is a major motivation for staff members to move out of their family homes. Workers' residential environments must have proximity to the studio or contractors, and their work conditions have a strong influence on their residential conditions.

5.2.3 Staff Work Habits

In the following subsections, the work habits of Studio M staff will be characterized through an analysis of their activities at the studio. Figure 5.3 shows the shift lengths and working situations of studio staff. According to C1, the animation picture staff schedules were full of tasks on the second day of the investigation because the whole studio was working on a "retake"[12] operation for a job, which was contracted as "gross" after the "all rush."[13] However, the working conditions of directors are more ordinary, even although each director handles different schedules because the tasks assigned to them are different (see Table 5.4). Figure 5.3 shows the obvious differences between the shift lengths of animation picture staff and those of directors.

5.2.3.1 Animation Workers

On December 15, the first day of the investigation, all of the animation picture workers left the studio at around 5:00 a.m. (with the exception of C4) to go home for a 24-hour rest period. They returned to the studio at around 7:00 a.m. on the 16th, and remained at the studio for the remainder of the observation, a period of about 41 h. The interviews revealed that this behavior is part of a pattern that repeats about once every 4–6 weeks, after an all rush, when retakes are requested and the animation picture workers at Studio M must work through the night to complete them.[14] The time required for the retake operations cannot be estimated until the all rush is held, but based on experience, C1 expected that the animation picture workers would have to work through the night for several days. C1 directed the animation picture workers to take a day off to rest before the retake operations began.

An animation picture worker's average working day outside of retake operations is 10 h long. Their working hours and break times are not strictly scheduled, but are left to the workers' discretion. They can only start work on a given project after the

---

[12]A "retake" is the application of a modification to drawings as requested by clients. The time allotted for a retake operation is typically about a week, though this sometimes varies depending on products and schedules.

[13]An "all rush" is a viewing attended by the director in charge of a project, the client studio, and the investors.

[14]The deadline period before the all rush and the retake period after the all rush are the busiest times for animation picture workers.

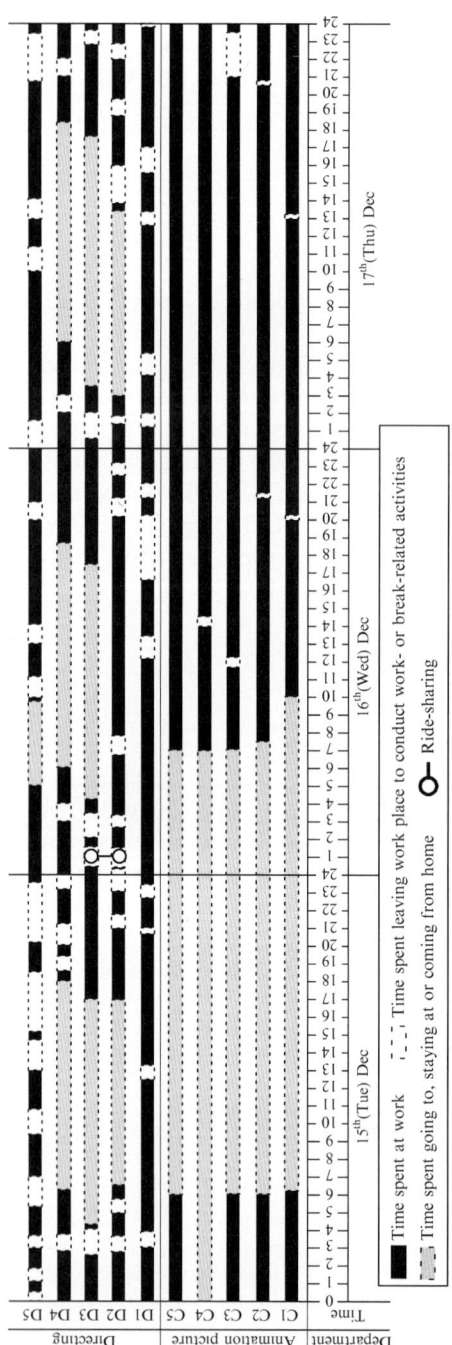

Fig. 5.3 Activities of the ten interviewees working at Studio M from 12:00 a.m. on December 15 to 12:00 a.m. on December 18. *Source*: Daily activity survey

Table 5.4 Studio M director
job descriptions in March
2010

ID	Jobs
D1	TV series A(#1, α)
D2	TV series B(#17, #20, β)
D3	TV series A(#10, α), TV series C(#51, γ)
D4	Sales, general affairs
D5	TV series A(#8, α), GM

Source: Interview survey
Note: "#" in Jobs represents an episode number in an animated series; Greek letters indicate client studios; "GM" indicates animation movie clips for a video game

upper processes are completed, and they often have to wait for half-finished products to be delivered from the upper processes (Fig. 5.2). Accordingly, the time that they spend waiting to start jobs is not insignificant. According to the interviews, animation picture workers usually arrive at the studio in the afternoon and depart on the day's last train. At times, some workers cannot finish their jobs in time to catch this train and end up sleeping at the studio.

During the investigation period, workers rarely left the studio for personal reasons. C3 went out to a restaurant for 2 h starting at 9:00 p.m. on the third day. Otherwise, there were only a few 30-minute trips to the nearest supermarket to purchase boxed lunches. However, although staff did not often leave, they did engage in various break-type activities aside from their main jobs such as taking naps, having conversations, and watching animated shows on DVD. They spent most of their working time at the studio with their coworkers.

Studio M does not provide introductory training per se for its workers, although workers do acquire skills through on-the-job training in some opportunities such as guidance from senior workers, departmental training, technical school, and independent study. The departmental training is provided by C1, and all five of the animation picture workers also have friends or coworkers in the studio who coach them or give them advice.[15] Conversation among workers is important because it gives them a chance to exchange advice and coach each other. In a working environment where workers spend long hours together not only working, but also eating and taking breaks, there are many opportunities for new arrivals to acquire skills and develop new techniques.

5.2.3.2 Directors

Some of the directors, namely, D2, D3, and D4, returned to their homes two or three times during the investigation period. All three lived within walking distance or within a 30-minute drive by motorbike. They left the studio between 3:00 a.m.

---

[15] Two interviewees answered that friends from nonanimation industries are their other choices.

Fig. 5.4 Studio M directing department in the middle of the night. *Note*: Not only project proposals, scripts, and storyboard books but also many comic books and novels are kept at hand as the originals for animation; here they can be seen on the right desk. The director sitting in front of the left desk watches an animation product streaming on a video Website. Many figurines and toys can be seen in this photo

and 6:00 a.m., and usually returned to the studio between 5:00 p.m. and 7:00 p.m. (Fig. 5.4). D1 did not go home during the investigation, and D5 went home once for only 5 h.

D1 and D5 indicated why they did not go home more often. D1's answer was as follows: "I do not have time to go home during busy periods. I have restaurants and convenience stores near the studio and a place to sleep at the studio so I do not bother to go home." D1's sleeping place is a napping area provided by Studio M for workers who do not or cannot go home (Fig. 5.5). Both D1 and D5 took naps or slept at the facilities during the investigation.

D5's answer was as follows: "I thought about going home several times, but it is dangerous to drive after working all night, and so I did not." It takes 50 min for D5 to reach the studio by motorbike or car (a studio-owned car), and D5 usually was not sufficiently alert and rested to drive during the busy period. D5 did go home from 5:00 a.m. to 10:00 a.m. on the second day of the investigation. D5 took a 3-hour nap, and then delivered a job to a freelance animation picture worker.

The frequent trips observed during the late evening are also a characteristic pattern among animation picture workers. Except for trips home and D2 and D3's

Fig. 5.5 Studio M napping facility. *Note*: This simple napping facility consists of a sofa, a sleeping bag, and a body pillow in a corner of the studio

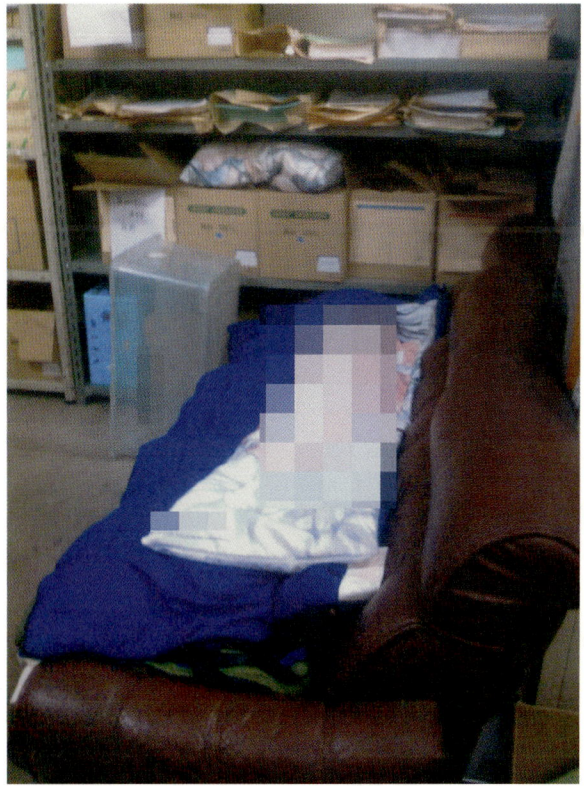

outing for dinner on December 16 at 1:00 a.m., the destination of all trips was to freelancers or contracted studios. Eighty-eight percent of workers' destinations, excluding their homes, were located within 10 km of Studio M, and their travel times were often short, between 30 min and 1 h. The purpose of these visits to freelancers and contracted studios is to meet with and deliver half-finished products to business partners. Some were round trips to and from a single partner while others were multidestination trips to several partners before returning to the studio (Fig. 5.6).

The directors determine the destinations of their trips according to their discretion and the projects they handle. Each destination can be visited by (1) several workers or (2) only one particular worker. Studio α's order of Studio M's TV series A was an example of type (1). D1, D3, and D5 handled the production of TV series A and frequently visited Studio α[16] (see Table 5.4). These trip patterns indicate that Studio α is the major transactional partner for Studio M.

Studio M also engages in business relationships of type (2), such as the partnership between D2 and Studio β, and that between D5 and several creators. According to the interviews, Studio β appoints D2 when it orders a job from Studio M because the person in charge at Studio β likes D2. D2 lists the proximity to that specific

---

[16] D1 visited Studio α two times, D3 visited one time, and D5 visited seven times.

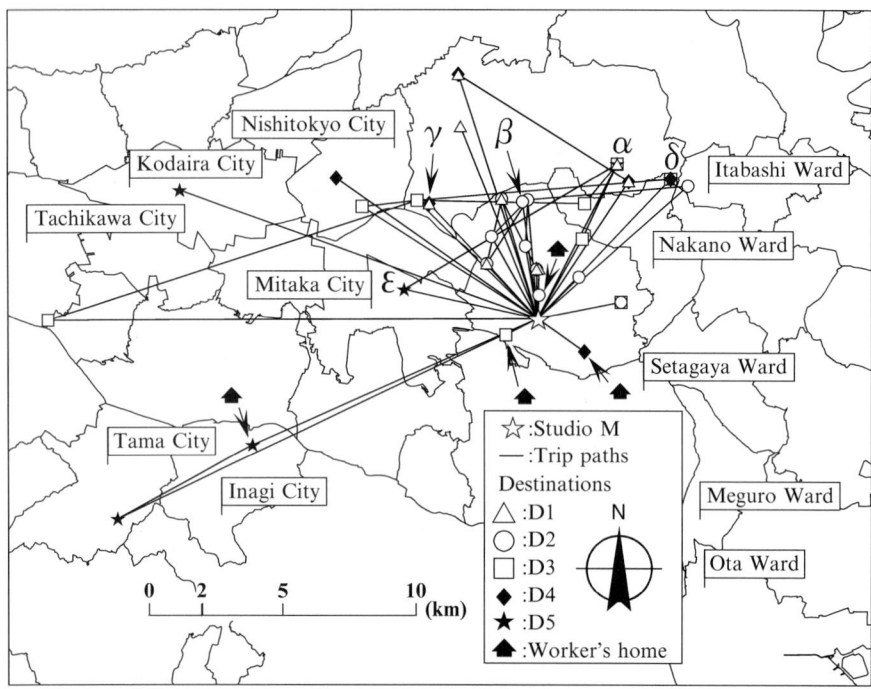

Fig. 5.6 Range of directors' daily activities. *Greek letters* stand for the same client studios as in Tables 5.3 and 5.4. D1 through D5 are worker IDs. *Source*: Daily activity survey

partner as a reason for choosing D2's current residence; this fact indicates the depth of the relationship between D2 and Studio β. D5 lists the proximity to the creators from whom D5 orders jobs as a reason for choosing D5's current residence (Table 5.3).[17] These facts indicate that Studio M's type (2) transactions include studios or creators with whom the directors have built friendly relationships.

In many cases, directors build their own personal networks with studios or creators outside of Studio M's business networks, and they allocate jobs flexibly depending on the requested quality and the available schedule.

The opportunities available for directors to acquire skills at work are similar to those for animation picture workers: directors also learn the skills they need for handling projects through on-the-job guidance from senior workers, technical schools, training offered by the studio, and independent study. However, three of the five directors said that they had no senior workers who could give them advice, while one of the directors listed a friend at the studio as an adviser. Directors tend to have fewer advisers than animation picture workers. The primary job of the

---

[17] One of the subcontract studios that D5 hires is run by a sole proprietor whom D5 calls "*Shisho* (Master)." Because D5 is deeply impressed by the quality of this creator's work and Shisho's productivity, D5 provides jobs to this creator preferentially.

directing department is the management of project schedules, which includes placing work orders, transportation of half-finished products, arrangement, and so on. These skills can be acquired through advice from senior workers or through training held by the studio. However, projects handled by different directors have situations that vary depending on the preferences of the client, the specific workers involved, the progress of the entire project, and other factors. As a result, it may not be straightforward for one director to advise another; rather, flexibility and quick thinking are important. This aspect of their work may contribute to the fact that directors have fewer advisers.

5.2.3.3 The Case of One Director: D5

Figure 5.7 shows the observed activities of D5. According to the interview with D5, the first half of the investigation (from 11:30 p.m. on the 14th to 7:00 a.m. on the 15th) covered a usual busy workday for D5, but the latter half (from 7:00 p.m. to 11:30 p.m. on the 15th) was extremely busy because of the all rush.

The primary jobs D5 was doing were different in the first and second halves of the investigation, as reflected by the increased workload in the second half. In the first half of the investigation, most of D5's time was spent on transportation of half-finished products and communication with workers at Studio M. In the latter half, D5 did not transport any products, but instead spoke by telephone with workers at other studios and freelance creators and had meetings with workers at Studio M. D5's job had shifted from progressing along with the schedule to adjusting to the schedule as the deadline loomed.

Trips (totaling 261 min) occupied the largest segment of D5's activities during the investigation, and four of the five trips were for the transportation of half-finished products. D5 spent the second longest segment of time (217 min) on communication with workers both in the studio and at other studios or freelance creators. The time spent on communication regarding adjustments to the production schedule can

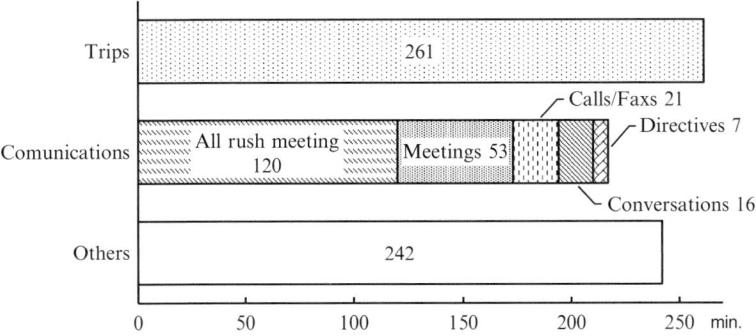

Fig. 5.7 Time spent by D5 (from 11:30 p.m. on December 14 to 7:00 a.m. on December 15 and from 7:00 to 11:30 p.m. on December 15). *Source*: Active observation

be broken down to meetings, calls/faxes, and directives (81 min), scheduling the all rush meeting (120 min), a conversation about nonbusiness matters, and a salutation meeting with the head of a directing department at Studio α (a 2-minute conversation). The topics of D5's 81 min of communication regarding the schedule adjustment varied depending on the channel of communication, such as direct face-to-face communication or non-face-to-face communication (e.g., telephone and fax).

Of D5's non-face-to-face communications, telephone conversation typically lasted 2–5 min, with topics mostly limited to a single matter. Two were about rescheduling the all rush meeting, one confirmed the direction taking for solving a problem, two confirmed the progress of a project, and two were regarding a deadline announcement. In addition to these calls, D5 also received a call from a freelancer whom D5 informed of the deadline and sent a fax confirming the progress and the deadline to a subsidiary in China. Overall, D5's non-face-to-face communications were simple conversations with workers at other studios or freelancers involving confirmation or adjustment of schedules and problems. D5 did not spend a large amount of time on non-face-to-face communications.

In contrast, D5's face-to-face communications were longer and encouraged advanced information sharing between workers. The purpose of D5's face-to-face communications was mainly exchanging opinions about the quality of products, and reaching consensus on various matters such as requesting other directors for support, reporting progress to the chief director, and arranging a quality management meeting with a coloring worker, a supervisor of key pictures, and animation picture worker C1. The periods of time spent on these communications ranged from 2 to 30 min, with longer conversations often occurring during meetings. For example, a meeting with a coloring worker and C1 was 30 min long, and a meeting with a supervisor of key pictures and a coloring worker was 15 min long. These meetings had not been scheduled previously, but D5 requested them after checking the quality of the products. D5's confirmed the progress, adjusted the schedule, and asked participants about the quality of half-finished products.

D5 lacks the drawing skills of an animation production worker and has not acquired any specific knowledge required to check the quality of products. Rather, he directs meetings and asks for advice on the quality of half-finished products from animation workers with professional skills and knowledge. D5's influence on the project schedule, which is based on the opinions D5 obtains at such meetings, cannot be underestimated.

5.3 Conclusion

According to the previous studies, the presence of various clusters of cultural industries and creative persons produces creativity in a metropolis. Some studies, backed up by qualitative data, have focused on studios as places for information exchange, which enhances creativity and aids in the development of new social networks. However, previous discussions of the roles of studios in workers' lives are still not sufficiently detailed to paint an accurate picture of communication within networks or to show how workspaces affect the creativity and behavior of workers (see Sect. 1.2.2). Thus, this chapter employs a time-geographical method to trace the activities and behavior patterns of end workers in the animation industry. The analysis of these activities affords a discussion about the studio workspace as a "creative nexus." A creative nexus is a place that offers support for creative work and where creative persons can do this work.

The subjects of this analysis are end workers in the animation industry. Some are workers in the production department and some are workers in the directing department. These end workers, who belong to the "core," produce creative materials for their studio's project, and the studios, their creative nexuses, in turn provide them with "convenience" by supporting their activities. In fact, the workers try to reduce time constraints by using fast-food restaurants or supermarkets close to the cooperative studio and napping facilities provided by the studio. The studio provides not only physical convenience, but also opportunities for building social networks, acquiring skills, and exchanging information.

The workers in the production department usually stay at the studio for several days during peak periods. These animators learn their skills through communication with colleagues and senior workers at the studios. Some workers from the directing department also stay at the studio for long periods so that they can receive quality checking reports or opinions about the products from animators extemporaneously and make instant changes to the project schedule. When a project is ongoing, these animators and directors share the same working hours, mostly from late evening to morning. The presence of sleeping accommodations within the studio and the use of fast-food restaurants might be the conditions that best support the creative activity at studios because these amenities allow the workers to pay little attention to their working hours and to work through the night without needing to go home. The studios enable creative workers with various skills to work at any time, which means that interaction between technical specialists and workers from different specialty departments is happening constantly.

In Tokyo, these creative nexuses are located fairly close to each other. While the activities of animators may be limited to the interiors of their studios, directors often leave their studios to make short trips to other studios. Directors use the studio's partners and their own acquaintances as contractors. These business relationships cause workers and studios to agglomerate into relatively small areas near other workers and studios because it is important for workers, especially directors, to access transactional studios and creators in short time periods in order to manage schedules effectively.

This network of creative nexuses and the communication between creative persons within these nexuses are important factors enabling creativity within the industry. These physically and socially proximate relationships are built within and among creative nexuses and are formed and maintained through the daily face-to-face communication of creative persons. These types of networks and the working environments of creative workers encourage the animation industry to agglomerate in the metropolis of Tokyo.

References

Arai Y, Okamoto K, Kamiya H, Kawaguchi T (1996) Toshi no Kukan to Jikan: Seikatsu Katsudo no Jikan Chirigaku [The space and time of cities: the time-geography of daily activities]. Kokonshoin, Tokyo (Japanese)

Arai Y, Nakamura H, Sato H, Nakazawa T, Sugizaki K (2004) Multimedia and Internet business clusters in central Tokyo. Urban Geogr 25:483–500. doi:10.2747/0272-3638.25.5.483

Bain AL (2004) Female artistic identity in place: the studio. Social Cult Geogr 5:171–193. doi:10.1080/1464936041000169020 4

Bain AL (2005) Constructing an artistic identity. Work Employ Soc 9:25–46. doi:10.1177/0950017005051280

Blair H (2003) Winning and losing in flexible labour markets: the formation and operation of networks of interdependence in the UK film industry. Sociology 37:677–694. doi:10.1177/0038038503037400 3

Hara S (2005) Gurobaru Kyoso Jidai ni okeru Nihon no Dejitaru Kontentsu Sangyo Shuseki no Kyoso Yuisei to Inobeshon no Hokosei - SD Gandamu Fosu Purojekuto o Jirei ni [Competitive advantage and innovation of digital content industrial clusters in Japan in global competition era: a case of "SD GUNDAMFORCE" project]. Ann Jpn Assoc Econ Geogr 51:368–386 (Japanese)

Japan Institute for Labor Policy and Training (2005) Kontentsu Sangyo no Koyo to Jinzai Ikusei: Animeshon Sangyo Jittai Chosa [Employment and human resource development in contents industry: actual condition survey of animation industry]. The Japan Institute for Labor Policy and Training, Tokyo (Japanese)

Scott AJ (1988) Territorial reproduction and transformation in a local labor market: the animated film workers of Los Angelse. In: Metropolis. The University of California Press, California

Statistics Bureau, Ministry of Internal Affairs and Communications (2012) Shakai Seikatsu Kihon Chosa 2011 [Survey on time use and leisure activities 2011]. Statistics Bureau, Ministry of Internal Affairs and Communications, Tokyo (Japanese)

Stoper M, Venables AJ (2004) Buzz: face-to-face contact and the urban economy. J Econ Geogr 4:351–370. doi:10.1093/jnlecg/lbh027

The National Tax Agency (2010) Minkan Kyuyo Zittai Tokei Chosa [The statistical survey of actual status for salary in the private sector 2009]. The National Tax Agency, Tokyo (Japanese)

Throsby D (2001) Economics and culture. Cambridge University Press, New York

Vinodrai T (2006) Reproducing Toronto's design ecology: career paths, intermediaries, and local labor markets. Econ Geogr 83:237–263. doi:10.1111/j.1944-8287.2006.tb00310.x

Chapter 6
Promoting the Animation Industry in Local Regions: A Case Study of Working Conditions at an Animation Studio in Okinawa

Abstract This chapter examines the conditions necessary to promote the growth of the animation industry in local regions through a case study of an animation studio in Okinawa. The investigation specifically focuses on the background behind a Tokyo studio's decision to establish an Okinawa branch and the cooperation between these two related studios. The government of Okinawa Prefecture implemented a promotional policy to support their local industry. The Okinawa studio was required to collaborate with local industries to create new employment and generate industrial development through the production of an animated film. Daily working hours and workdays at the studio had to be regulated at the Okinawa animation studio because the studio was run with governmental support. However, Tokyo studio staff regularly work through the night. The Okinawa studio was unable to communicate rapidly enough with the Tokyo studio to produce animation and lacked much of the technology used by the Tokyo studio. Hence, the Tokyo studio's extensive experience and access to technology ensured that they were responsible for a large part of the production.

Keywords Division of labor • Local regions • Okinawa • Policy • Working environment

6.1 Introduction

6.1.1 Context

The Japanese animation industry is one of the content industries that have agglomerated in East Asian metropolises such as Tokyo, Seoul, and Shanghai.[1] Among the studios in these cities, divisions of labor networks have developed,

---

[1] For example, 79 % of animation studios in Japan are located within Tokyo, and 37 % of these studios are agglomerated specifically in Nerima and Suginami wards. In addition, the contractors or partners of animation studios also agglomerate in Tokyo (see Chap. 2 for more information).

© Springer Japan 2014

K. Yamamoto, *The Agglomeration of the Animation Industry in East Asia*,
International Perspectives in Geography: AJG Library 4,
DOI 10.1007/978-4-431-55093-8_6

and the causes prompting this development correlate with the evolution of the animated film industry. The factors involved in the formation of successful international relationships include differences between the various cities' levels of industrial development, networks among production studios and managers, and regional policies that favor industrial investment (see Chaps. 3 and 4).

The extant transactional relationships among East Asian countries, in which South Korea and China act as subsidiaries for Japanese productions, have shifted under the effects of recent economic and political changes. For example, the demand for animated videos and TV shows targeted at the Japanese domestic market, the products leading sales in this industry, have decreased since 2006. In South Korea, on the other hand, production aimed at the South Korean domestic market as well as investment in that market has grown as a result of political support; consequently, the proportion of subcontracted production from overseas has decreased (see Sect. 3.2.2). Domestic demands for animated products in China have also increased because overseas productions cannot legally be broadcast during prime time (see footnote 4 in Chap. 4). In the Japanese content industry, some local governments have encouraged the growth of the industry in their own regions through strategies such as promoting locally produced animation products, promoting tourism to animated film fans, and encouraging social interactions between local people (Masubuchi 2010; Yamamura 2011). The practice of animation tourism or "*seichi junrei* (pilgrimage)," wherein animation fans visit places modeled in animated films, has attracted attention from local governments and local private organizations. In response, these local governments have implemented industrial promotion policies aimed at attracting investment by and further local development of content industries, which is expected to benefit local tourism, related industries, and the local economy.

This chapter examines the promotion of the animation industry in local regions based on an analysis in Okinawa, Japan. The Okinawa studio that is the subject of this analysis was established as a subsidiary of Studio M (the studio studied in Chap. 5) in the 2000s. In this chapter, a comparison is made between working conditions at the studios in Okinawa and Tokyo. In the first section, an overview of Studio M's situation and the policies in place in Okinawa Prefecture at the time when the Okinawa studio was established will describe how and why the Okinawa studio came to be. The subsequent section details the establishment of the Okinawa studio by Studio M and compares the working environments in each studio. Finally, we discuss some means of promoting the animation industry in local regions.

6.1.2   Methodology

In 2009, the Okinawa studio was established with 26 employees as a subsidiary of Studio M. Studio M, by comparison, was established in 1986 and employs 36 people. The basic characteristics of Studio M staff, such as payment systems, average working times, monthly salaries, and other basic features of Studio M appear to be typical, as they are similar to those of the studios detailed in The Japan Institute for Labor Policy and Training (2005) and in Chap. 2.

Our investigation of the working conditions at the two studios was performed according to the same method used in Chap. 5. In each location, the investigation period covered three successive days, from December 15 to 17, 2009, at Studio M, and from January 5 to 8, 2011, at the Okinawa studio. The same questionnaire used in Chap. 5, which was influenced by that of Arai et al. (1996), was employed in the present investigation to establish the basic staff characteristics. The questionnaire items, covering such topics as payment system, educational background, and job history, were also used in the author's previous studies. Ten workers from Studio M and nine workers from the Okinawa studio participated in the investigation. Two additional questionnaires were administered in October 2011 and from September 2012 to February 2013 to complement the research.

The dates of the investigations in Tokyo and Okinawa were more than 1 year apart, and the investigation in Tokyo was not centered on a production period. Nevertheless, the interview clearly shows the characteristics of daily activities at Studio M. Activity analyses lasting 1 or 2 days were performed for three workers at the Okinawa studio. This type of analysis of the daily activities of end workers in a creative industry was not found in previous studies to the best of my knowledge. Although Chap. 5 has already documented the results of the investigation of Studio M, this chapter refers to some of that data because it is necessary to compare the workers' activities between the Tokyo and Okinawa studios to enhance our understanding of the structure of agglomeration.

6.2   Establishment of the Studio and Industrial Promotional Policies Aimed at the Okinawa Animation Industry

Studio M and the government of Okinawa Prefecture were both involved in the establishment of the Okinawa studio, but the two had different purposes. In accordance with the research by Yamamoto (2012), this section will describe how and why the Okinawa studio was established.[2]

In 2001, Studio M, the parent studio of the Okinawa studio, established a subsidiary in Wuxi, China (hereafter the Chinese studio), to increase productivity, satisfy demand in the Japanese animation market, and reduce production costs in the lower processes (animation pictures and coloring).

Although this subsidiary was expected to function as a division of the animation picture and coloring departments in the Studio M group, Studio M was burdened with the operative issues that came with its subsidiary, such as a rise in labor costs and the sluggish growth of staff skills. At Studio M's Chinese subsidiary, the cost of producing an animated picture in 2009, the year the Okinawa studio was established, was greater again by half compared with that in 2001. In addition, the manager at Studio M experienced communication difficulties with the Wuxi studio because of differences in business customs. The business partnership with the Wuxi

---

[2] Detailed information can be found in the example of Studio B in Yamamoto (2012).

Fig. 6.1 Okinawa studio animation picture department. *Note*: Okinawa animation workers receive training in animation picture work from the quality inspector from Studio M

studio had been sustained by the low labor costs available in China and by the high demand for Japanese animation products. However, this demand decreased in recent years and the Wuxi studio's performance no longer satisfied the needs of Studio M. Given this situation, Studio M established a new animation studio in Okinawa in 2009. The aim of the studio in Okinawa is to exploit a new market and eventually to take over part of the production process from Studio M (Figs. 6.1 and 6.2).

Okinawa Prefecture has a high unemployment rate[3] and the lowest minimum wage[4] in Japan. In response, the local government of Okinawa Prefecture has implemented some new industry policies to generate employment. The new subsidiary studio was established in Okinawa in part to receive subventions from one such policy.

---

[3] According to "the 100 Index of Okinawa, 2011 version" by Okinawa Prefecture (http://www.pref.okinawa.jp/toukeika/100/100_index.html, Accessed on April 12, 2014), the unemployment rate in Okinawa in 2009 was 7.5 % compared with 5.1 % for the rest of Japan. The ratio of job offers to job applications in 2008 was 0.38 in Okinawa compared with 0.88 in all of Japan.

[4] According to the Ministry of Health, Labour and Welfare's document "List of minimum wages by prefecture" (http://www.mhlw.go.jp/seisakunitsuite/bunya/koyou_roudou/roudoukijun/minimumichiran/index.html, Accessed on May 5, 2012), the minimum wage in Okinawa is 645 yen compared with the 737 yen national average and was one of the lowest wages in Japan, along with Iwate and Kochi, in 2011.

Fig. 6.2 Okinawa studio coloring department

This policy is an emergency employment measures project created by the Ministry of Health, Labour and Welfare for encouraging business collaboration to create new industry and employment.[5] The project's expense totaled 180 million yen, and four entities were chosen as recipients: a contracted company such as a travel agency from another prefecture, an advertising agency in Okinawa, a dance school, and the Okinawa studio. The Okinawa studio was assigned about 38 million yen. More than half of the subvention was paid as salaries, and the rest was spent on producing animation.

In this project, the Okinawa studio collaborated with local industries to create new employment and industrial development. In March 2011, their product was broadcast throughout Okinawa Prefecture. Figure 6.3 shows the region on which the fictional town in the 25-minute animation was modeled. This region incorporates several towns, mainly on the southern part of Okinawa's main island. The Okinawa studio produced this animated short to assist the tourism industry and collaborated with regional industries to provide images of characters for the product packages of a food company and advertising posters in convenience stores.

---

[5] The business entities were chosen by the public and a review board. The Okinawa studio moved into the startup incubator facility at Uruma City. Though the manager of the studio did not specify an amount, he said that he rented two-thirds of the facility's second floor for a bargain price.

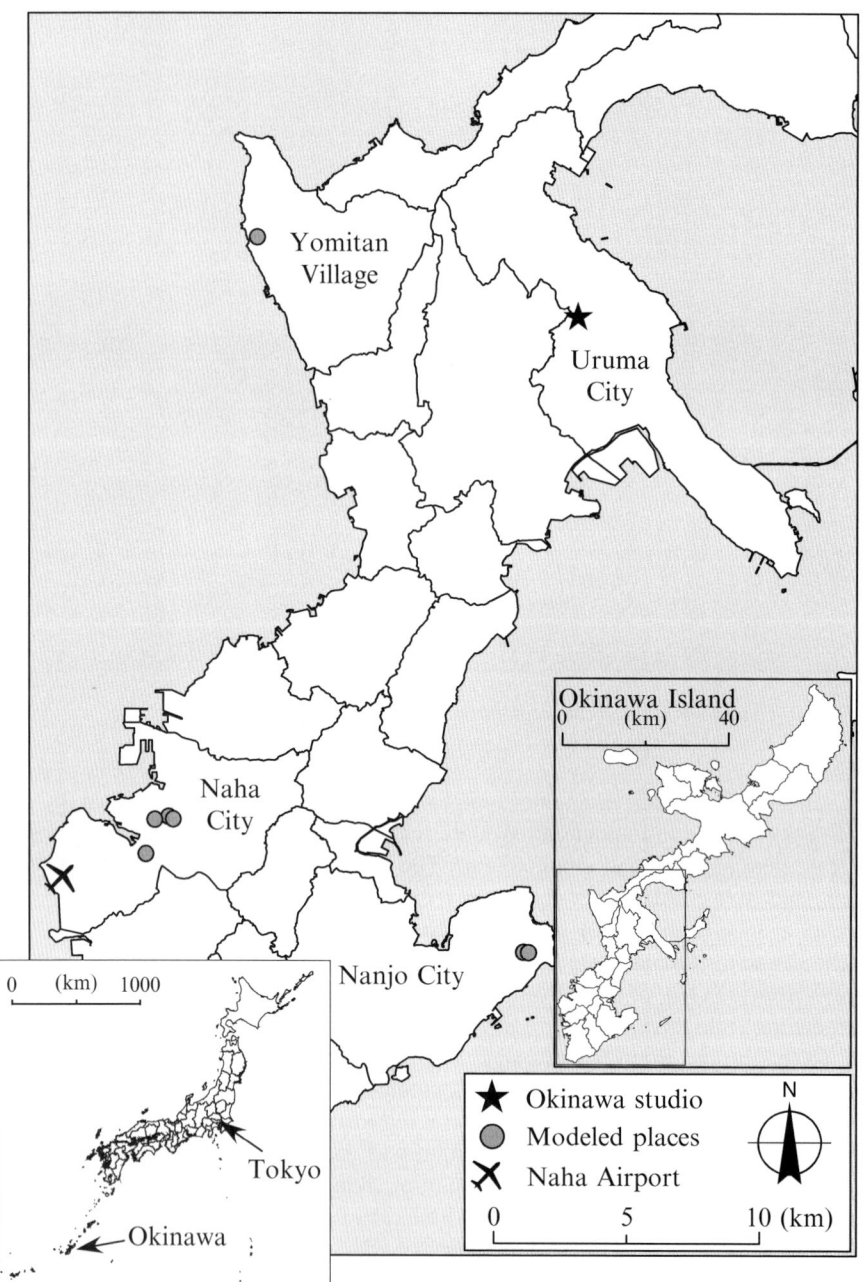

Fig. 6.3 Location of the Okinawa studio and nearby places modeled in the animated film produced there. *Note*: Naha is the capital city of Okinawa Prefecture. *Source*: Interview survey

6.3 Working Environments of the Okinawa Studio and Studio M

6.3.1 Basic Staff Characteristics

All interviewees at the Okinawa studio were end workers, belonging to the animation picture or the coloring departments, both of which are lower processes. However, interviewees at Studio M were chosen from among five workers each from the animation picture and directing department. The main task of the directing department is the management of production schedules and the transportation of half-finished products between animation studios. Directors' job skills, therefore, are quite different from those of production department workers (see Chap. 5).

In the case of Studio M, four out of the five production staff are freelancers and their wage system is based on delivered results. The fifth worker is the head of the department, who supervises the quality of the drawings and the education of new animators. Studio M employs the worker at a fixed salary to motivate the worker to stay in this position rather than asking for a promotion. All of the directors at Studio M are employed on a regular, fixed payment system. Employment as a freelancer or pay based on delivered results can be regarded as the typical employment system in the production departments in the animation industry, as mentioned in Chap. 2. In the animation industry, each product requires a labor force of different quality and quantity, and productivity is heavily dependent on staff skills. As it would be prohibitively expensive for animation studios to offer year-round employment to all of the productive staff needed at peak times, it is logical for animation studios to flexibly employ freelancers.

In contrast, all of the Okinawa staff are contract employees and their payment system is a combination of base salary and commission. It is easier for the Okinawa studio to estimate its required workforce because of its supportive role in Studio M's work. At the same time, it is hard for the Okinawa studio to employ regular workers on a permanent basis because each project is based on a temporary contract. As a result, the Okinawa studio cannot guarantee long-term employment. Thus, all staff at the Okinawa studio are employees with 1-year contracts.

An analysis of staff academic backgrounds shows that four of the nine participating Okinawa studio staff and five of the ten Tokyo studio staff had graduated from technical schools. These data show that most workers have learned basic animation techniques before they obtain their jobs in the industry. Although staff at the Okinawa studio and Studio M have similar academic backgrounds, these similarities have different meanings for them. Because Tokyo has many studios, it also offers more opportunities for employment.

Animation industry workers in Tokyo point out the abundance of studios and chances for employment as one of the reasons why they live in Tokyo (Chap. 2). In Okinawa, in contrast, Studio M's subsidiary is nearly the only studio that can employ animators. Thus, the Okinawa studio provides an important chance for potential animators to demonstrate their skills.

6.3.2   Studio Working Hours

Figure 6.4 indicates the interviewees' activities while working at the studios. Production staff in Studio M mostly stayed at the studio, except on the first day when they went home to rest in expectation of working late the next day. They have meals stocked at the studio for days when they have to stay in for prolonged periods. During the investigation period, they worked on a "retake," which requires them to work day and night modifying their drawings. According to a Studio M production worker, these retake projects occur about once a month. However, even outside the retake period, animation picture staff can and do come in to work at any time—day or night.

However, directing department staff come to the studio at around 6 p.m. and make several trips in the course of the night, at the end of which they either go home or stay at the studio. The purpose of these trips is to transport half-finished products to partner studios or to hold meetings with partners or creators. A directing department worker pointed out that working at night is convenient because other studios also work the same hours and because transportation at night is smoother because of reduced traffic (See also Chap. 5).

However, at the Okinawa studio, staff are typically at the studio from around 11 a.m. to 8 p.m., and unlike Studio M staff, they stay at the studio throughout their working hours. Because there are no shops near the studio, Okinawa studio staff either buy their meals from lunchbox distributors or bring their own lunchboxes. The difference in working times between the Tokyo and Okinawa studios is not simply because of a difference in the ratio of their staff professions such as production or directing. The working hours at the Okinawa studio must be kept to "reasonable" limits because the studio is supported by the local government of Okinawa Prefecture as part of a policy aimed at generating new employment in the area. According to a producer directing a project at the Okinawa studio, a flexible working-time system was adopted for all workers at the studio, with an exception being the prohibition of working after 8 p.m. When workers need to work late, their working hours after 8 p.m. are treated as overtime. In fact, some interviewees who worked more than 8 h in a day and/or after 8 p.m. clearly wrote "overtime work" on their survey sheets. Others intentionally spread out their working time across several days to avoid exceeding the specified hours (Fig. 6.5). Such behaviors are not seen among Studio M staff.

6.3.3   Limitations in the Division of Labor

Table 6.1 lists the activity areas of the staff who participated in creating the animated TV program produced and broadcast by the Okinawa studio in March 2011. Some public officers of the prefectural government, such as the head of the industrial policy division, were involved in the planning of the program. The directing

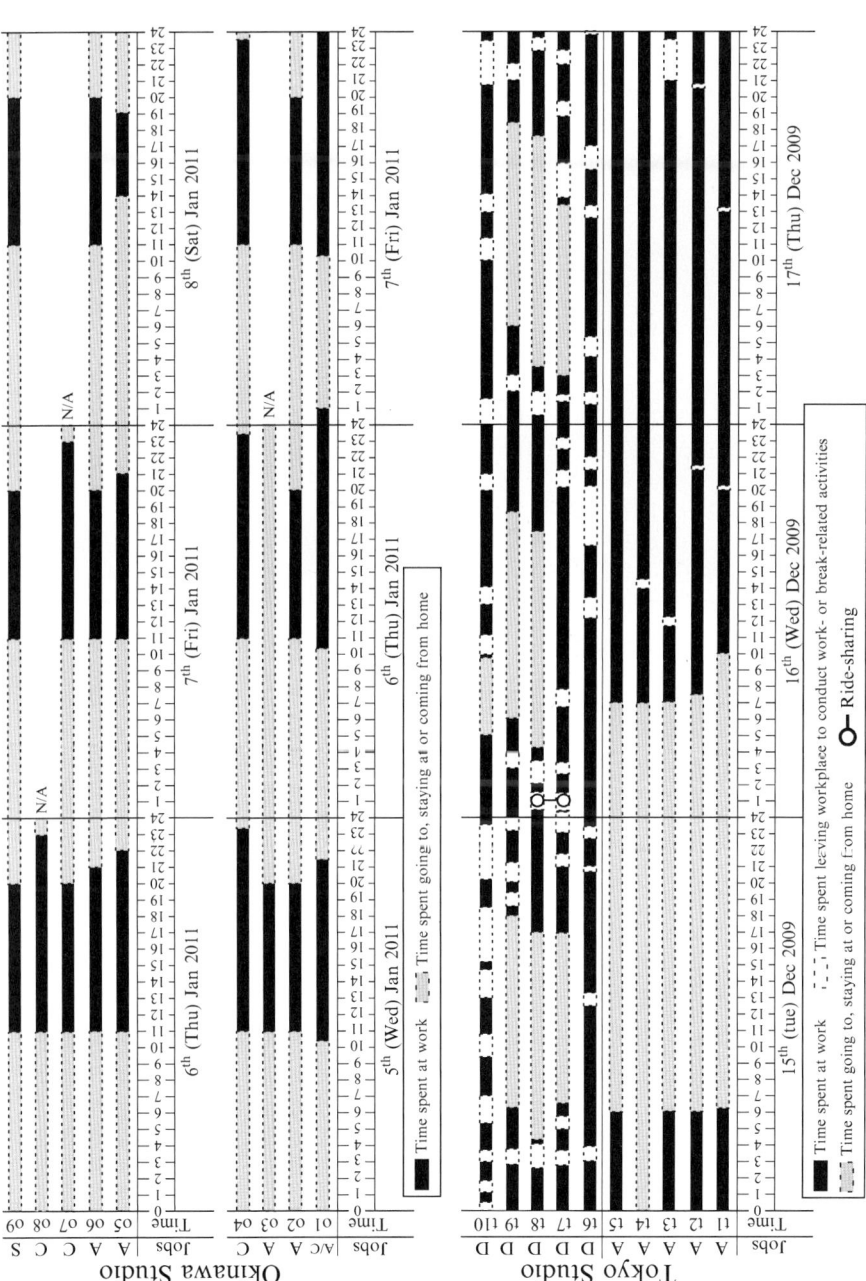

Fig. 6.4 Working day for Tokyo and Okinawa studio staff. *Note*: In the Jobs column: *A* animation picture, *C* coloring, *D* directors, *S* shooting. *Source*: Daily activity survey and interview survey

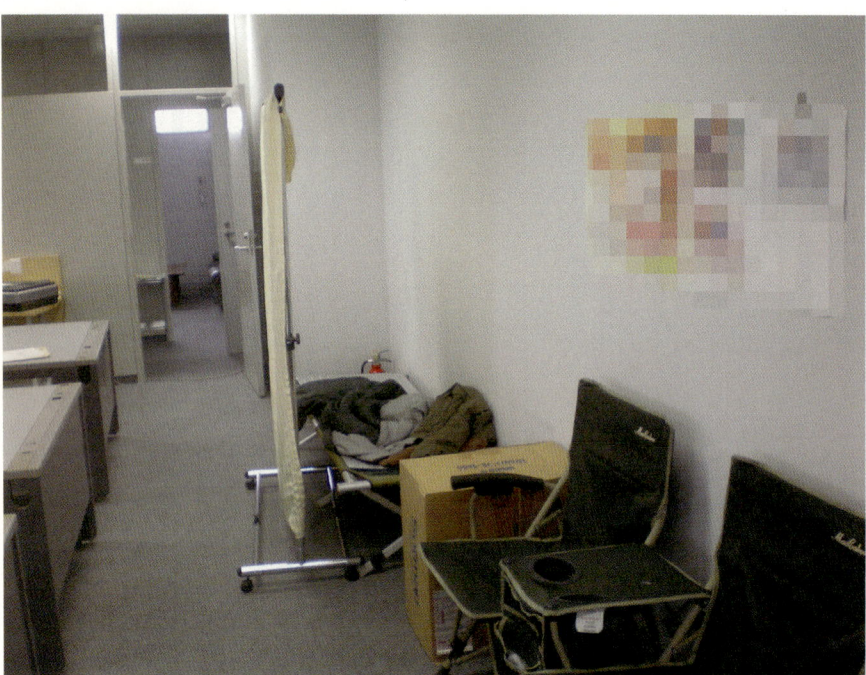

Fig. 6.5 Okinawa studio napping facility. *Note*: Okinawa animation studio staff had to go home every day. This facility was used by a supervisor

Table 6.1 Placement of staff

Job fields	Tokyo	Okinawa	China	Others
Producer	3	1	–	–
Planning	–	12	–	–
Scripter	1	–	–	–
Supervisor	–	1	–	
Key picture	19	1	–	3
Animation picture	2	9	Unknown	–
Coloring	–	4	Unknown	–
Background	11	–	–	–
Sound	4	–	–	–
Voice actor	2	10	–	–
Shooting	6	–	–	–
Editor	3	–	–	–
Recording	2	–	–	–
Director	5	5	–	–
Total number of organizations	18	2	1	1

Source: Credits of the animated show produced in part by the Okinawa studio and interviews survey
Note: "Total number of organizations" shows the total number of organizations and studios to which staff belong. The number shown in the table includes freelancers who did not belong to any studio. "Planning" is consisted of public officers of the prefectural government

jobs were performed by workers who had migrated from Tokyo to Okinawa. Voice actors were chosen by the people of Okinawa, with the exception of two professionals from Tokyo. However, the core production processes such as key pictures and backgrounds as well as the postproduction processes such as editing and sound were all handled by Tokyo studio staff.

Compared with Studio M, the Okinawa studio has more staff in its animation pictures and coloring departments. Nevertheless, the productivity of the Okinawa studio is only 60 drawings per day, which cannot satisfy the project's requirements.[6] Accordingly, most of the animation pictures and coloring were contracted to the Chinese subsidiary of Studio M.[7] In addition, it was not feasible for the Okinawa studio to accumulate the necessary expertise and arrange suitable facilities for voice recording in the short time available. Therefore, the voice actors (selected by the general audition) living in Okinawa needed to visit Tokyo for recording purposes.

A director[8] in the directing department at Studio M and a producer of animated shows cited communication difficulties as the cause of this tough situation and the project's limited success. Telecommunication is difficult between the Tokyo and Okinawa studios because of the differences in their working hours. The Okinawa studio also has a shorter working day, which means that it is hard for the Tokyo staff to catch the Okinawa staff at the office in the event that flexible changes to the product are required. To implement such changes, other studios such the Tokyo and Chinese studios are handy because it is easy to transport half-finished products to other studios in Tokyo and to secure a greater volume of production within a shorter period with the Chinese studio.

In the year and a half since its establishment, the Okinawa studio has not accumulated sufficient techniques or facilities to produce a single episode of an animated film by itself and must hence share its production process with other cooperative studios. However, because the animation industry has agglomerated in Tokyo, the Okinawa studio cannot find any other studios with which to cooperate and share work in its region. Although Studio M, which is the parental studio of that in Okinawa, is the only studio with which the Okinawa studio has a reliable connection, communication difficulties between the Tokyo and Okinawa studios remain unsolved. As a result, the animators at Studio M and those in China, at the other subsidiary of Studio M, took over the bulk of the production from the animators at the Okinawa studio, who had fewer accumulated skills and less productivity.

---

[6] Although the productivity of the Okinawa studio is not high, it is often necessary to transport half-finished products between the Studio M and Okinawa studios. This transportation is realized by a package service and through the Internet. File transfer protocol is used for electronic transportation of products, especially for colored animation pictures.

[7] Because the number of staff at the Chinese studio is unknown, the productivity of the animation picture and coloring departments is given as 900 sheets of paper per day.

[8] This director is worker t7 in Fig. 6.4.

6.4   Conclusion

This chapter has discussed the potential for industrial promotion in the animation industry at the level of local cities based on a case study of the Okinawa studio and the governmental policies on which it is dependent. The findings are summarized below.

The industrial promotional policies are beneficial for Okinawa Prefecture because they provide jobs to workers who have few employment opportunities, but have learned basic animation skills. These policies also benefit Studio M by allowing them to better exploit the labor market and reduce their production costs.

Even though some technical schools for animators are located in Okinawa, the animation industry there is underdeveloped, which means that graduates of the local technical schools cannot find jobs in their region. The Okinawa studio may be able to recruit these hidden workers. The tapping of these human resources is the other benefit of this project.

Nevertheless, it is hard to conclude that the Okinawa studio has expectedly functioned as a source of continuously produced content. This is partially because the Okinawa Prefecture government provided not only support to the studio, but also some restrictions, especially regarding working conditions and the allotted time for technical training.

Because of the necessity of learning and accumulating technical knowledge, it is difficult to train skillful workers in a production process in the animation industry when only a short time period is allotted to training. The Okinawa studio is still in its early stages, but it has no cooperative studios in its neighboring regions. Under the added limitation that their governmental support would expire after only 1 year, it has been almost impossible for the Okinawa studio to sustain all of its business activities, which range from training to the production and broadcasting of animated products. Moreover, the Okinawa studio has not been able to secure cooperation from other studios because of the differences in working hours between Okinawa and Tokyo, which makes it difficult to build synchronized communication between studios, such as in face-to-face communication and telecommunication.

With its low levels of technical accumulation and productivity, the Okinawa studio could not fulfill its intended roles and required tasks. Eventually, the majority of the production shifted back to Studio M and its network, both of which have created and sustained many animation productions in the past.

To avoid the difficulties faced by the Okinawa studio and to promote the growth of the animation industry, local cities must provide not only infrastructure, such as electronic communication, which allows the delivery of products and instructions through internet, but also working conditions that include employment rules and working hours that enable flexible and instant communications with other studios.

In 2011, the Okinawa studio was dissolved because of its deteriorated finances. However, the former Okinawa studio staff and a producer in Tokyo established a new studio in Okinawa in December 2012. It will be necessary to observe the development of this studio to further assess the growth of the Okinawa animation industry.

References

Arai Y, Okamoto K, Kamiya H, Kawaguchi T (1996) Toshi no Kukan to Jikan: Seikatsu Katsudo no Jikan Chirigaku [The space and time of Cities: the time-geography of daily activities]. Kokonshoin, Tokyo (Japanese)

Japan Institute for Labor Policy and Training (2005) Kontentsu Sangyo no Koyo to Jinzai Ikusei: Animeshon Sangyo Jittai Chosa [Employment and human resource development in contents industry: actual condition survey of animation industry]. Roudou Seisaku Kenkyu Houkokusho 25 (Japanese)

Masubuchi T (2010) Monogatari o Tabisuru Hitobito: Kontentsu Turizumu toha Nanika [People who travel in the story: What is contents tourism?]. Sairyusha, Tokyo (Japanese)

Yamamoto K (2012) Animeshon Sangyo no Bungyo Kankei to Chiiki Seisaku [Division of labor in animation industry and regional policy] In Ito T and Yanai M (ed) Sangyoshuseki no Henbo to Chiiki Seisaku – Gurokaru Jidai no Chiiki Sangyo Kenkyu [The changes of industrial agglomerations and regional policies: the studies of regional industries under glocal era], Minerva shobo, Tokyo, pp 195–215 (Japanese)

Yamamura T (2011) Anime/Manga de Chiiki Shinko: Machi no Fan o Umu Kontentsu Turizumu Kaihatsu Ho [Regional promotion by Anime and Manga: the development method of content truism for making fans of the town]. Tokyohore shuppan, Tokyo (Japanese)

Chapter 7
Generalities and Regionality Observed in the Agglomeration Structure of the Animation Industry in East Asia

Abstract In this chapter, the generality and regionality of the agglomeration of the animation industry in three metropolises are expressed by knitting the findings of the previous chapters together. The important factors promoting the agglomeration of the industry include the agglomeration of related content industries that include the animation studios' major clients, the need for flexible and instantaneous division of labor between studios, the presence of a flexible and specialized workforce in a particular area, and highly developed social networks among workers. At the same time, the large domestic market and the presence of animation technical schools scattered throughout the country push the Japanese animation industry toward regionality. In Seoul and Shanghai, studio locations differ according to business practices and the demands of major clients. In Shanghai, these locations are regulated by policy as well. The animation industry in East Asia is agglomerating in metropolises through the interaction of these generalizing and regionalizing forces.

Keywords Agglomeration • East Asia • Generalities • Regionality

7.1 General Factors Leading to the Agglomeration of the Animation Industry

The preceding chapters have indicated that the general factors leading to the agglomeration of the animation industry include the regional concentration of related content industries, which supply the major clients for the animation industry market, the need for flexible and instantaneous division of labor between studios, and the self-reinforcing concentration of the skilled workforce in particular areas. This chapter shows how these factors promote agglomeration.

© Springer Japan 2014   139
K. Yamamoto, *The Agglomeration of the Animation Industry in East Asia*,
International Perspectives in Geography: AJG Library 4,
DOI 10.1007/978-4-431-55093-8_7

7.1.1 Regional Concentration of Major Clients and Related Content Industries

The major clients of the animation industry are related content industries, such as TV stations and the advertising, publishing, and game creation industries.

In Tokyo, animation studios can be categorized into two types: primary contractors that manage the scheduling of animation production projects, and professional subcontractors that specialize in particular production processes. The primary contractors have transactional relationships with related content industries, and they receive most of their orders from these sources. When an order is received for an animated series to be broadcast on TV, face-to-face communication between the primary contractors and clients occurs frequently in the form of weekly meetings. The animation industry is mostly sustained and developed by domestic demand. The proximity to domestic clients is important for the primary contractors, and this contributes to their tendency to agglomerate in Tokyo. Similarly, even though the domestic markets for animation in South Korea and China are small, animation studios tend to agglomerate in Seoul and Shanghai because they also seek transactional relationships with and proximity to related content industries.

Research shows that studios in Seoul conduct business transactions with the multimedia production industry and the advertising industry; as such, they require geographical proximity to these industries and easy access to their information. Studios in Shanghai, by contrast, have TV stations as their major clients, and some studios conduct business with publishers based on the merchandising rights of overseas clients.

Although the major clients of studios in these three metropolises belong to different content industries, proximity to the relevant content industries, which tend to agglomerate in metropolises, in the hopes of increased transactional opportunities is one of the major determinants of studios' site selection in all three cities.

7.1.2 Flexible and Instantaneous Division of Labor with Other Studios

Several production processes are required for studios to produce animated films, and labor-intensive processes are necessary in the production departments, especially the animation picture and coloring departments. Moreover, as any delays introduced into the production schedule during the upper processes have to be absorbed in these lower processes, the animation picture and coloring processes must be completed quickly. To achieve this, studios often subcontract some of their work to other animation studios, which would not be possible without physical proximity. When many studios are clustered close together, each studio can choose the other studios with which it will place its orders, depending on the characteristics of the products and the requested deadline. This is why studios need proximity to other studios; this need promotes agglomeration.

In Tokyo, relationships between studios have matured so that studios can recruit workers for immediate jobs and technical needs on a daily basis. Small studios have built nonexclusive relationships with other studios, and the transactions they receive are floating rather than regular and fixed. Studios do not insist on written contracts because they prefer to prioritize flexibility and instantaneous communication rather than time-consuming guarantees of the details of each contracted job. Only the customs of the animation industry ensure the stability of these unwritten transaction agreements. The mutual trust between studios is critical in established through repeated transactions.

These relationships based on mutual trust are built between business managers who were once associates or colleagues. Studios in Seoul build similar relationships through which they overcome the skilled labor shortage by sharing technical professionals with each other. Such neighboring studios recognize themselves as peers and share a tacit understanding that each will keep away from the other's clients.

Transactional relationships that build on mutual trust between studios also operate in Shanghai. Some of the Shanghai studios choose subcontracting partners based on necessary skill sets. Studios spun off from other studios handle such specialized processes and frequently engage in transactions with other studios to complement their own workforce and staff skills. Human networks and shared history in the industry, such as that between two managers who formerly worked together at the same studio, guarantee the credibility of these relationships as well as the ordering studios' promise to pay, and the contracted studios' promise to deliver the requested product.

In these three countries, the flexible and instantaneous division of labor with other studios is essential to the production of animated films, and is sustained by transactional customs within the industry built upon mutual trust between studios.

7.1.3   Flexible, Specialized Workforce

Animation industry staff have specialized skills that are necessary for animated film production. Studios must flexibly organize workers who are good at producing the particular type of animation or atmosphere needed for a particular production, such as 3D computer graphic science fiction or pastel-hued fairytale imagery. Studios are always on the lookout for new workers in this highly specialized workforce and agglomerate in metropolises partly for this reason.

The Tokyo animation industry workforce flexibly supplies workers, mostly freelancers, with sophisticated skills to studios. These workers learn their techniques through on-the-job training and advance their careers by working jobs they obtain through their human networks of friends and acquaintances. These human networks are also important means for workers to avoid job instability. Thus, animation workers' personal networks provide both training opportunities and work referral contacts, and so represent an extremely important element in a successful career. The need to maintain these social relationships compels workers to agglomerate in

Tokyo. Career formation made possible through workers' human networks is a driving force in sustaining the flexible and specialized workforce in the animation industry.

Career formation in the animation industry has various directionalities depending on the region. In Seoul, most workers are freelancers who flexibly sustain the productivity of the industry. They use human networks to avoid job instability in two ways. The first is the acquisition of technical expertise through coaching from superiors and training with colleagues. The second is career development through gaining experience at several studios and learning multiple skills. Human networks built between workers with different specialties further encourage the agglomeration of workers, which in turn enables the development of more specialized workers.

In contrast to studios in Tokyo and Seoul, studios in Shanghai hire workers as regular employees rather than freelancers. However, their payment systems are based on completed output or commissions, which indicate that the job situations of workers in Shanghai are as unstable as those in Tokyo or Seoul. In other words, the Shanghai studios flexibly control the labor supply by adjusting their pay. From the workers' viewpoint, human networks are just as important as in Tokyo and Seoul. Workers learn skills at studios from superiors and through training, and obtain jobs through colleagues and friends.

These human networks encourage the development of a self-replicating workforce within the animation industry. Workers agglomerate in metropolises so that they can find jobs and develop their careers. They improve their skills to satisfy the technical requirements of the studios, and studios hire workers flexibly and provide job opportunities. This is the process by which a specialized and technically skilled workforce is sustained in the metropolis.

7.2 Regionality of Agglomeration in the Animation Industry

The circumstances surrounding the animation industry differ between these three metropolises. This section identifies some characteristics of each region.

In Tokyo, the most notable regional peculiarity is the large size of the domestic market. The stable management of studios is strongly dependent on transactions with related content industries, which means that proximity to related domestic content industries is more critical to studios in Tokyo than to those in the other two regions.

The other remarkable regional characteristic is the existence of numerous animation technical schools that supply new workers to the Tokyo studios. Some studios send their workers as lecturers to animation technical schools, where they also scout for talented students. Students wishing to work in the animation industry learn the necessary skills before employment. Neither Seoul nor Shanghai has schools that supply new workers. Most new workers have received no technical education before employment and must find their own opportunities to acquire the necessary skills.

One characteristic common to both Seoul and Shanghai is their shared dependency on overseas markets. The domestic markets in South Korea and China are not large enough to sustain native industries, and most transactions are made with overseas clients. Because of the small size of the domestic markets, it is important for studios to protect their business opportunities with overseas clients. One way in which they can do this is through temporal proximity to these clients, which they achieve by agglomerating in areas close to international airports.

Overseas clients influence not only the site selection of studios, but also the structure of the industry and the agglomeration process. Clients from different countries tend to require different quantities and qualities of animation products, so studios must specialize. Especially in Seoul, technical workers with particular specialties form their own labor pools around studios, and agglomerations of studios with particular specialties can likewise be observed within the city.

For example, Japanese studios often order products with rapid turnaround times from studios in Seoul, where a complementary workforce helps to produce the required work. For the requested product to be delivered within the prescribed deadline, the South Korean studios must use advanced techniques in special processes. Western clients, however, tend to emphasize product quality and studio location. Studios with Western clients therefore emphasize the reputations of their neighborhoods and the quality of their products rather than their short delivery times. In addition to their transactional relationships with clients, Seoul studios also build relationships among themselves to recruit complementary workforces with the right mixture of technical capabilities. To maintain the quality and uniformity of their products, studio staff follow jobs through multiple processes. It is therefore necessary for workers to acquire multiple skills; accordingly, they set up learning opportunities, such as training meetings with coworkers, on their own.

In the Shanghai region, subcontracted processes are limited to production departments under the international division of labor between the client country and China. As the production departments require an abundant workforce, it is very important for Shanghai studios to possess a workforce of the right size as well as temporal proximity to their clients.

The distribution of studios in Shanghai does not suggest that the studios' site locations were chosen based only on the needs of the client countries. Rather, site selection must have been influenced by Shanghai's remarkable regionality, maintained through governmental policies and regulations aimed at industrial promotion in certain areas. In China, private ownership of land is prohibited whether by individuals or corporate entities. Thus, site locations do not reflect studios' decisions; instead, they are strongly influenced by government provisions. However, the studios intentionally choose Shanghai for their headquarters because Shanghai provides them with business opportunities with its external economy. Shanghai satisfies studio needs because it provides industrial infrastructure, easy access to overseas clients, and a rich workforce.

The Chinese government has high expectations for the development of the animation industry and has implemented industrial promotional policies in several cities, including local cities such as Wuxi, which is located 160 km west of Shanghai and is one of the major industrial cities in the Yangtze delta. Some of the animation studios in Wuxi are subcontractors for the Japanese animation industry. This work is enabled by Wuxi's proximity to the Shanghai international airport, governmental support, and the presence of a cheap workforce. Dependence on overseas transactions and political implementation has led to the agglomeration of the animation industry in Wuxi.

7.3   Division of Labor Among Regions: The Role of Studios and Their Worker Networks

The practice of the division of labor among regions has developed as part of the animation production process. Its development has been promoted by the rise of informatization. Yet the division of labor is limited to relatively simple jobs such as the animation picture process and the coloring process. It is important for the creative department, which requires frequent synchronous communication through face-to-face contact, that any subcontractor has a working environment and culture similar to their own, including working hours and business styles.

Therefore, some subcontracted studios engaged in division of labor relationships with clients in other regions align themselves with the transaction rules and working hours of the major client and parent studios located outside the region. For example, some Seoul studios build and maintain their relationships with Japanese partner studios by embracing Japanese business culture. Some have also developed complementary collaborative work-sharing relationships with other studios located in their neighborhoods, outsourcing when their workload demands it. The reason why Wuxi became an investment destination for Japanese studios is that the Wuxi studios can operate at times that satisfy Japanese production practices. However, the Okinawa studio had a strong cultural link to the Tokyo studio, but the working hours and production capabilities there were regulated according to the demands of the local government because it was supporting the studio. As a result, a successful creative collaborative relationship could not be built between the Tokyo and Okinawa studios.

Animators work at any given hour both within and around the Tokyo studios. They actively communicate with coworkers through conversations and impromptu meetings. Some workers, especially directors, build far-reaching networks including workers at other studios. Therefore, mutually complementary transactional relationships are well developed around the Tokyo studios.

The development of these relationships indicates that the studio is not only a workspace for creative workers, but also the place where they shape their imaginations through social networking. A studio fulfilling these roles is called a creative nexus in this book. Creative nexuses are agglomerating in the western suburbs of Tokyo, and these nexuses are connected to each other through the human networks of their workers. These networks consist not only of business partnerships, but also of social relationships, such as master–disciple relationships.

As above, we argue that the agglomeration of the animation industry is driven by complex networks operating on various spatial scales, from those within indivisuals to regional scales. These relationships promote the agglomeration of the animation industry in metropolises.

7.4 Contributions and Future Approaches

This book focuses on the animation industry and its agglomeration structure. Our study involved a microscopic survey based on traditional Japanese economic geographical methods, yet also demonstrated macroscopic issues, such as the fact that the international division of labor is based on the assumption of a wage gap between industrial and developing countries.

There is room for argument regarding the spatial relationships between studios' transactional relationships and the behavioral characteristics of their staff, as shown in previous studies of the content industry. While the present study is limited to the animation industry, it sheds light on the relationships among participants on various spatial scales, including regions, studios, and individuals. The idea that both generality and regionality are factors in the agglomeration of the animation industry, as shown in the division of labor among regions, the nature of the transactional relationships among studios, and the characteristics of workers' behaviors, contributes to an understanding of the studios' location choices and the agglomeration structure of the content industry in general.

Saxenian (2006) called managers who had worked in Silicon Valley and then returned to their home countries "Argonauts." Saxenian pointed out that the management expertise and business culture that they imported from Silicon Valley gave the new IT industrial agglomerations in their home countries an internationally competitive advantage. The present study identified Seoul, South Korea, and the Shanghai region in China as participants in the international division of labor in the Japanese animation industry. Animation studios in these metropolitan regions have not only agglomerated in particular regions, but also adopted the transactional customs and industrial structures of their major client countries. For example, some studios in Seoul and the Shanghai region doing business with Japanese clients have embraced Japanese-style transactional customs: they might design their facilities to look more like those of their Japanese clients, use transactional sheets for production or employ Japanese speakers in the studio. These studios were able to connect with Japanese partners and also to transact with other studios located nearby, but using the same Japanese customs. Although not all of the managers at these studios have necessarily worked in Japan, they are familiar with the Japanese rules of business. Thus, as importers of an advantageous foreign business culture, they can be compared with the Argonauts.

Some animation studios do not explicitly record contract details so that they can ensure flexibility of their contracts' contents. This is an example of a characteristic custom among Japanese-style animation studios. Business agreements are instead based on mutual trust, which Williamson (1983) expressed as mutual monitoring relationships among peers. However, these trustful relationships are also maintained through mutual assistance. Some studios in Seoul share their subcontracted workloads with neighboring studios because of the need to use particular materials such as Japanese-made celluloid and paint or because of the short schedules that are sometimes demanded by Japanese clients. In addition, some Seoul studios continue to make unprofitable transactions with Japanese studios because they feel they owe the Japanese studios, while others take great care not to steal Japanese studios that are clients of other studios. These behaviors in business cement mutual trust relationships among animation studios, even across national borders.

Previous studies of industrial agglomeration have pointed out the importance of customs such as a flexible and specialized division of labor formed by firms in local areas to enable the diversification of demand (Piore and Sable 1986) or the reduction of production costs (Scott 1988); the importance of the local milieu (Camagni 1991) or regional network-based industrial system (Saxenian 1994) for facilitating transactional relationships, the importance of cooperative systems for nurturing innovation, and the importance of learning by region (Florida 1995) and collective learning (Capello 1999) for accumulating and utilizing knowledge and techniques (see also Chap. 1). The observation of animation workers yielded concrete examples of Florida's "creative class" (2002) and Throsby's "core" (2001) workers.

Creative workers are continually building networks among peer workers through daily face-to-face communications; through these networks, they find jobs and acquire skills. Many different abilities and roles, and therefore many workers, are required to run a creative project. The various workers involved in a project communicate directly and instantly with each other to produce one creative product. The reasons that workers give for continuing to work in Tokyo have to do not only with the agglomeration of the studios as the spaces for their creative activities, but also with the proximity of their coworkers. Therefore, creative workers of various kinds gravitate toward metropolises, and creative workforces self-perpetuate there as well.

In this book, the international division of labor relationships among small studios that do not necessarily have capital ties is shown through a field survey of the animation industry. These relationships are sustained by internal structures that promote agglomeration, such as the division of labor among peer studios and the constant development of new creative workers in each region. It is noteworthy that this book, although it is a case study of an industry, draws an integrating spatial structure among global, local, and personal relationships. This book also notes that the self-perpetuating structure of the workforce as realized through social relationships among the workers is a factor promoting agglomeration. At this point, this book offers the new perspective that workers and their daily activities are also among the important elements in promoting the agglomeration of a particular industry such as animation. In addition, this study contributes to agglomeration theory by redefining agglomeration as the formation of a network of creative nexuses where personal relationships are built in a limited space.

There are two possible future directions for this research. The first possibility concerns the division of labor relationships among regions other than Japan, South Korea, and China, as some Japanese studios transact with Indonesian studios, while the major clients of South Korean and Chinese studios include studios in the United States, Europe, and Japan. This finding suggests that the international division of labor structure is a worldwide phenomenon and is not exclusive to East Asia. Perhaps East Asian studios doing business in division of labor relationships with Western studios can be found to have adopted Western business customs, as indicated by the Seoul case study.

The second possible direction is to examine agglomeration in related content industries. This study has shown that functional concerns dictate the location of the agglomeration of the animation industry in metropolises, as shown through the frequent transactions and strong relationships between related content industries and the animation industry. Some animation studios in Tokyo transact with publishers and video game developers as well as broadcasting services. Some studios in Shanghai demand merchandising rights in the domestic market when they tender contracts with overseas companies. The industry is likely to take advantage of mixed media with related content industries, so that animation products will have a major economic effect not only on the animation industry, but also on related industries. Future studies must reveal more details of these relationships, including the frequency of transactions and shipments to the location of transactions, to better understand the agglomeration structure of the content industry as a whole in the metropolis. In other words, it is debatable whether the way in which this kind of creativity is sustained through the mutual influence between the space and workers in the animation industry in Tokyo can be applied to other creative industries or to industries in other metropolitan cities. A further exploration of case studies is necessary before that argument can be made.

References

Camagni R (1991) Introduction: from the local 'milieu' to innovation through cooperation networks. In: Camagni R (ed) Innovation networks: spatial perspective. Belhaven Press, London

Capello R (1999) Spatial transfer of knowledge in high technology milieux: learning versus collective learning processes. Reg Stud 33:353–365

Florida R (1995) Toward the learning region. Futures 27:527–536

Florida R (2002) The rise of the creative class. Basic Books, New York

Piore MJ, Sable CF (1986) The second industrial divide: possibilities for prosperity, Reprintth edn. Basic Books, New York

Saxenian A (1994) Regional advantage: culture and competition in silicon valley and route 128. Harvard University Press, Massachusetts

Saxenian A (2006) The new Argonauts. Harvard University Press, Massachusetts

Scott A (1988) Flexible production systems and regional development. Int J Urban Reg Res 12:171–186

Throsby D (2001) Economics and culture. Cambridge University Press, New York

Williamson OE (1983) Markets and hierarchies. Free Press, New York

Index

© Springer Japan 2014
K. Yamamoto, *The Agglomeration of the Animation Industry in East Asia*,
International Perspectives in Geography: AJG Library 4,
DOI 10.1007/978-4-431-55093-8

Printed by Printforce, the Netherlands